Let The Good Times Roll!

Let The Good Times Roll!

Nunc Pede Libero!

A Memoir of
Family, Friends & Crazy Days

by Kurt Krauss

Cover Designs, Graphics Layout, and "Fast Eddie"
by Bill Krauss

LET THE GOOD TIMES ROLL!
NUNC PEDE LIBERO!

iUniverse books may be ordered through booksellers or by contacting:

iUniverse
1663 Liberty Drive
Bloomington, IN 47403
www.iuniverse.com
1-800-Authors (1-800-288-4677)

Because of the dynamic nature of the Internet, any web addresses or links contained in this book may have changed since publication and may no longer be valid. The views expressed in this work are solely those of the author and do not necessarily reflect the views of the publisher, and the publisher hereby disclaims any responsibility for them.

Any people depicted in stock imagery provided by Thinkstock are models, and such images are being used for illustrative purposes only.
Certain stock imagery © Thinkstock.

ISBN: 978-1-5320-1345-4 (sc)
ISBN: 978-1-5320-1346-1 (e)

Library of Congress Control Number: 2016921208

Print information available on the last page.

iUniverse rev. date: 12/23/2016

This book is dedicated to my family: my wonderful wife, Bonita; my terrific children, Katie, Anna, and Joseph; my future son-in-law, David; and my treasured grandchildren, Aidan, Sadie, and Cam. You guys make life worth living.

Contents

Acknowledgments

S pecial thanks to Anna Krauss for pushing me to write this book. Thanks to Becky Eberts for telling me to listen to Anna. Thanks to everyone else for leaving me the hell alone. Thanks to Gloria, Bonita, and Katie for reading the first draft. Thanks to Cousin Bill for the design creativity and for drawing nice pictures.

Thanks to all of the players: Frank and Celene Varasano, Larry Roth, Jack and Mary Ann McGrath, Bonita Krauss, Bob Morin, Matt McKenna, Gary and Susan Shows, Gordy and Judy Ramseier, Walter and Becky Jewett, John and Laila Smith, Katie Krauss, Gail and Gloria Hamilton, Walter Wyse, Jim and Alicia Bachman, Ron and Connie Comer, Bill and Connie Krauss, Bill and Nona Greene, Anna Krauss, Joseph Krauss, Aidan Maguire, Sadie Maguire, James Taylor, John Belushi, Bobby Short, George Shearing, Brian Torff, Harry and Donna Thompson, Howard Cosell, Lou Rawls, Dusty Baker, Tom Seaver, Bryant Gumbel, Jim Scibelli, Lorne Michaels, Sir Paul McCartney, Jane Krauss, Bob Woolery, Ann Aldridge, Anne Barnes, Galen Barnes, Larry Caliguiri, Michael Murphy, Ed Collins, Charlie Greene, Frank Jones, WCBS Football Announcers, Jeffrey Lange, Greg Selias, Sam Newara, Jim Farley, Sam Nunn, John Devereaux, Roy King, Mike Wheeler, Réal Melançon, Yankee staffers Louie, Rocco, Mary Ellen, Roberto, and Willie, Warren Sapp, Jack Nicholson, Jesse Jackson, Chuck Schumer, John Houseman, Margot Harley, Burt Reynolds, Katie's friend Jessie, Patti LuPone, Don Cogman, Susie Lisle, Adam Zauder, Joe Fisher,

Puff Daddy, Jennifer Lopez, George Tracy, Danny Sullivan, Whitey Ford, Eddie Ford, Booz Allen colleagues Ginny, Chris, Coleen, and Peggy, Tom Jones, Jim Wolf, John and Lorraine Rockwell, and my Suicide League pals.

And thanks also to my incognito buddies: Elmer, Hank Sain, Tom Phillips, Samuel Benedict, Bob Feller, Lars Halversen, Mr. Oh, Rob Reese, Wilbur Too Slick, Brad, the McKinsey Guy, Joe Nathan, Jim Meyer, Debbie Stovich, Richard Redville, DDS, Peter Rayburn, MD, Mona Carroll, Jerry Gold, Jim and Susan, Mel Tickets, Johnny Diddel, Ronnie Stevens, Bob Busker, Kirby Green, Jules Irving, MD, Susie, the bartender, Mike Steele, Sir William, Sir Edward, Ralph (the Welcher) Welch, Nurse Goodbody, Lennie France, Jason Schmidt, Chloe, Babs and Margie, Stu Winthrop, and Fred, the transvestite.

Regarding the Subtitle

I decided early on that I wanted to use the Latin translation for *Let the Good Times Roll!* as a subtitle. I thought this might give the book a touch of class and allow me to charge a few bucks more.

I tried to work out the translation from online Latin dictionaries and eventually came up with "Adprobo Decora Tempore Volvo!" Then, feeling a keen responsibility to my readers, I decided to get confirmation of my subtitle from a learned source. I researched respected academicians and found Dr. William Batstone, professor of Classics at The Ohio State University. I then e-mailed Dr. Batstone for advice and counsel.

Here is a paraphrase of his first response:

> An expression like "let the good times roll" is much more difficult to put into Latin than you might think. The problem is metaphor and metonymy: "good times" is a metonymy for, say, party, and "roll" is a metaphor since time does not roll. The way a Roman would say something like "let's have fun" would be much more literal. When Horace, the poet, wants the party to begin, he says "nunc est bibendum," meaning "now, let's get drunk." And then he says, "Now is the time to dance" or "Now I will get crazier than Thracian."

I played around with some options and e-mailed Will back: "I'm thinking that Horace's line from his 'Ode xxxviii': *Nunc Pede Libero!*—Now is the time to dance footloose!—might be a good subtitle. Do I have it right?"

Will was quick to respond:

> I think you're headed in exactly the right direction. It's from Horace. Anyone with Latin would recognize it, and it is short. The original includes the phrase *pulsanda tellus*: "nunc pede libero pulsanda tellus," meaning "now with foot free let the earth be struck." I like the shortened version.
>
> This line is from a poem celebrating Octavian's victory over Cleopatra and Mark Antony. So, party hardy is the theme. *Pede libero*: with free foot, yes footloose. But also with a foot free from fear of Antony and Cleopatra in a Rome that is politically free from the potential tyrant Antony. And *tellus* is not just the earth, but the earth personified as a nourishing deity, who becomes the drum for the dance as the dancers beat the earth. So there are religious, political, celebratory overtones.
>
> I think *Nunc Pede Libero* is just right.

Thank you, Professor Batstone.

Setting the Stage

Lou Gehrig was a New York Yankee mainstay from 1925 until 1939. He started 2,130 consecutive games, a major league record until 1995. He holds many career and single-season records and was one of the greatest players of all time. He was the first baseball player ever to have his number retired. Number 4 will live in Yankee history forever.

In 1939, Lou was diagnosed with amyotrophic lateral sclerosis (ALS), and retired from baseball. The Yankees designated July 4, 1939, as Lou Gehrig Appreciation Day at Yankee Stadium. Players, managers, owners, and politicians gave heartfelt speeches about "The Iron Horse." When it came time for Lou to speak, he walked to the podium, looked out over the crowd and said, "Fans, for the past two weeks you have been reading about the bad break I got. Yet today I consider myself the luckiest man on the face of the earth."

This is one of the classiest introductions to any speech that's ever been given. But while Mr. Gehrig may have considered himself the luckiest man on the planet on that day in 1939, as of 2017, there is a new man in town—Me! I often think that I must be the luckiest man on the face of the earth.

Okay, to be completely honest, Bill Gates is probably luckier than I am, and so are Warren Buffett, Bruce Springsteen, and LeBron James. Oh, all right; maybe one porn star, two tops. So I guess that I am just among the luckiest men on earth.

First and foremost, I have my family. My lovely wife of over thirty-seven years, Bonita, is my friend, my partner, my lover, and my confidant. She is beautiful and smart. She is caring. She is a world-class mother. I could not ask for more. I love her to pieces, as they used to say.

Then there are our three children: Katie is currently thirty-six and is a successful business executive in Denver. Anna is thirty-four and just finished her last semester of nursing school, which she hopes to combine with her training in yoga and Urban Zen to become a unique, multidisciplinary health care provider. She lives in Columbus, Ohio, with her fiancé, David Crossley, and their three children. Joseph is twenty-nine and also lives in Denver. He works in warehousing and distribution and is an accomplished gamer. All three of our children are thriving and succeeding. Each of them is doing interesting things, and they make us very proud.

Now we come to the grandchildren, or as I refer to them: the Yard Apes. Aidan, age twelve; Sadie, age nine; and Cameron, age ten, are our treasures. They are cool little people, and we thoroughly enjoy our time with them. We are able to see them a lot, which is important given how busy their parents are. We visit interesting places, we go out for Sunday brunch, we go to movies, and we have sleepovers. It's a joy to be with them and also a joy to see them go home, if you get my meaning.

If family is the number one reason that I'm so blessed, friends have got to be number two. There are undoubtedly folks that have more friends than Bonita and I have, but our friendships tend to run long and deep. Just for fun, I made a list of our twenty-five closest friends. On average, we have been friends with these people for twenty-five years. Five are over forty years; only two are less than ten years. We view friendship as a long-term proposition.

Our friends are the ones who created this book. They participated in all the high jinks described herein, and honestly, dreamed a bunch of them up. For some reason, we tend to attract wacky friends who are adventuresome and willing to try almost anything one time. They truly make life worth living.

After friends and family comes career. And again, I have been blessed to be at the right place at the right time. When I left college in 1971, I was lucky enough to land a job in manufacturing management, specifically production and inventory control. This was a discipline that was undergoing major, transformational change brought on by the availability and capability of the computer. I was privileged to get in on the ground floor of this work and built a national reputation in the field.

Then I decided to attend graduate school at Carnegie Mellon University, and received my master of science in industrial administration (CMU's MBA) in 1979. I spent two great years in Pittsburgh. The academics were challenging, and my friends were diverse and interesting.

Given my age and experience, I had the self-discipline to devote each weekday—morning, afternoon, and evening—to either class or studying. As a result, I rarely had anything to do on Saturdays and Sundays except play. And Bonita generally visited every other weekend. Life was good.

I had negotiated a deal with the dean of the Business School that awarded me credit for the business and teaching experience that I had gained before returning to school. This enabled me to graduate in only three semesters instead of the usual four. The summer before I graduated, I accepted a position with the blue-chip management consulting firm of Booz Allen Hamilton. We decided to forego a summer intern position and went straight to a permanent offer. I worked for four months during the summer of 1978, returned to school for four months, and then rejoined the firm in December.

My years at Booz Allen turned out to define my career. I loved management consulting, and I was pretty good at it. I started in the Cleveland office, moved to Atlanta in 1981, and ended up in the New York office in 1991. I was elected to the partnership in 1984, and I served on the firm's board of directors from 1988 to 1991. I led the firm's service operations practice for a number of years, and was the managing partner of the Atlanta office for several years. It was a hell of a run.

In 1992, I left Booz Allen. Two former partners of mine, Stefan Bard and John Smith, and I started our own firm. The Mead Point Group stayed together for five years, and the three of us had quite a time. We made more money, and we worked fewer hours. All of the administrative bullshit that comes from working with a big firm totally disappeared.

My largest client was Young & Rubicam, the global advertising agency. After trying to hire me for a couple of years, they made an offer to buy our firm in 1997. Y&R wanted to integrate strategic management consulting with the various marketing and communications services that they provided to clients, in the hopes of enhancing the quality and value of both.

My partners and I were ready for a new challenge, and after a few rounds of negotiations, we agreed to sell. We didn't get a lot of cash and we all took a reduction in salary, but we received a bunch of low-priced stock options in Y&R. This would prove to be a very good deal.

Shortly after I joined Y&R, the company uncovered accounting fraud at Burson-Marsteller, at the time the world's largest public relations and marketing communications firm—and Y&R's largest subsidiary. I had been working closely with the CEO of Burson, Tom Bell, for maybe two years on a major, strategic transformation of the business. Based on our work together, both he and the CEO of Y&R, Peter Georgescu, asked me to become chief financial officer of Burson-Marsteller. After a lot of back and forth, I finally agreed.

Boy, am I glad that I did. What a time it was. We got the fraud issues cleaned up pretty quickly and then started to build a world-class financial organization: great people, great culture, great systems, and great processes. And we succeeded beyond my dreams. Even though I was and still am a management consultant at my core, my three years as CFO of Burson-Marsteller were the best three years of my professional career.

In 1999 we took Y&R public, and the value of my options increased fourfold. Then, in 2000, we sold the agency to the WPP Group for $4.7 billion, and the value of my options increased tenfold. Driving home one night prior to the closing, I thought through our financial situation and determined that we had enough money for me to retire. I talked it over with Bonita, and she said, "Go for it!"

On October 3, 2000, the day after we closed the deal and six days shy of my fifty-first birthday, I retired. I had always dreamed of retiring at fifty. Now, my dream was a reality.

For the past sixteen years, I've had a ball. I have served on eight different boards of directors: multibillion-dollar public companies, private start-up companies, not-for-profit organizations, the gamut. I have taken up crossword puzzle constructing and, as of this writing, have had twenty-three puzzles published in the *New York Times*, the *LA Times*, and the *Wall Street Journal*. And now I've written a book. Life is great!

Bonita and I divide our time between Naples, Florida, and Columbus, Ohio. Naples has the sunshine. Columbus has the grandchildren.

We have also begun traveling around the United States and Canada every summer with some dear friends of ours: Ann Aldridge, Bob Woolery, Anne Barnes, and Galen Barnes. So far we have visited Alaska, Montana, Wyoming, the Upper Peninsula of Michigan, Vancouver, and the Canadian Rockies.

These trips are crazy fun. We all get along very well. There are lots of jokes and lots of laughs. Galen tends to be very deferential to the women, a behavior that elicits regular teasing from Bob and me. Bob is the world's most aggressive driver, and he always demands to be behind the wheel. That adds a certain roller coaster aspect to our trips. Anne, Ann, and Bonita are determined shoppers and are always plotting their next session of retail therapy. And I usually serve as the trip organizer and navigator. Unfortunately, I tend to catnap during long car rides, which has caused more than one missed turn. That drives Bob absolutely crazy and makes him drive even faster. Good times!

So there you have four of the five reasons why I am one of the luckiest men on the face of the earth: my family, my friends, my career, and my retirement. The fifth reason is simply all the crazy stuff that I have been able to get away with over the years. Whether it be pranks or put-ons or horseplay or gags or spoofs or rowdiness or plain old tomfoolery, I have had lots of occasions to just let the good times roll. And all the credit goes to the family, friends, colleagues, and strangers that you will meet in this book. They get the credit; I get the royalties.

This book is a collection of a number of anecdotes, all of them actual events that I have been part of over the years. All of them are good times. And all of them roll. I hope that you are entertained.

M eet Edmund, the Party Boy Elephant, known to his friends as Fast Eddie. He is the official spokesman of the *Let the Good Times Roll Society* and is responsible for spreading the word about the joys of a life with many good times and lots of rolling.

Fast Eddie will appear throughout the book to share his thoughts, experience, and ideas related to living the good life and letting good times roll. Pay close attention. Fast Eddie knows his stuff.

Family

I could care less if you lick the windows, take the special bus, or occasionally wet your pants. You hang in there; you're special!

The Dumbest Man on the Planet

I am a very lucky man. On June 3, 1979, I married the perfect woman. Well, maybe Bonita isn't perfect—but she's about as close as you can get. She is beautiful. She is sexy. She was and is a terrific mother. She created a beautiful home that served, and still serves, as a refuge for the entire family. She is thoughtful. She is kind. And she puts up with the likes of me. As you read these stories, try to imagine what it would be like to be married to a gadabout like me. Bonita is a saint in designer jeans.

As our thirtieth wedding anniversary approached in 2009, we thought it might be fun to celebrate with all of our children and grandchildren. And what better place to meet up than at the Wequassett Resort on Cape Cod in Chatham, Massachusetts, where we spent our honeymoon back in 1979.

Our children, Joseph, Anna, and Katie, and our grandchildren, Aidan and Sadie, met us at the Wequassett for three days and three nights of food, family, and fun. We are blessed that we have a very close family that really enjoys its time together. Everyone was in good form, and the trip was a blast. We had real fun making some wonderful new memories.

But my best memory of Cape Cod did not happen on that trip. It happened thirty years earlier, during our honeymoon. It involved meeting some famous people. And it involved feeling dumber than a stump.

One day during our honeymoon, we decided to visit Martha's Vineyard. It took about an hour to drive from Chatham to Woods Hole and then another forty-five minutes for the ferry ride from Woods Hole to Martha's Vineyard. As I recall, it was a beautiful June day on the Cape: sunny, dry, and temperatures in the seventies.

We spent some time walking around in Edgartown and found an art gallery named Christina's. Inside we found some terrific paintings by an artist named Thomas Pradzynski, a Pole who studied and lived in Paris. He called himself an urban realist. We fell in love with his work and bought one piece on that first visit. Over the years, we have continued to collect his work. Today, we have ten of his paintings.

After the art gallery, we had lunch at a quaint little French restaurant. And after lunch, we decided to do what many Martha's Vineyard visitors do: rent mopeds. We found a dealer and rented two scooters for the afternoon.

What a time we had. We made a giant loop around the island and saw almost all the sights. The scenery was amazing, and the ocean views were breathtaking. We rode for maybe two hours to the far western point of the island, where we decided to take a rest. In the town of Aquinnah, there is a neat spot called the West Basin Boat Ramp. It's very quiet and secluded, so we decided to stop there for a midafternoon break.

We parked the mopeds, sat down on the retaining wall, and dangled our feet in the water. Talk about heaven on earth. We sat there by ourselves for quite a while until our solitude was interrupted by the arrival of a noisy, old Willys Jeep. There was no boat being trailed by the Jeep, but the driver backed straight down the boat ramp almost into the water.

Then we got a big surprise. Who should climb out of the Jeep but John Belushi and James Taylor? This was at the height of John Belushi's popularity: he'd been on *Saturday Night Live* for four years and *Animal House* had been released ten months earlier. Similarly, James Taylor was also at the peak of his popularity. We were impressed.

We walked over to them and introduced ourselves. They tried to do the same, but we said, "Yeah, yeah. We know who you are."

We asked them what they were doing at the boat ramp, and JT said, "We're getting salt water for a big clambake that we're hosting this evening."

They then proceeded to fill three fifty-five-gallon plastic garbage cans with salt water and manhandle them into the back of the Jeep.

When they were finished, they walked back over to us.

"James," John said, "have you ever ridden a moped?"

"No, I never have. How about you?"

"Nope."

Then James said to us: "Hey, guys. Can we borrow your mopeds and try them out for a while?"

Most of the time, I am sort of a "throw caution to the wind" kind of guy. Seize the moment. Grab life by the throat and don't let go. But I also have exactly two risk-avoidance genes that exert themselves from time to time. This was one of those times.

I looked Mr. Taylor right in the eyes and asked, "So what do we do if you don't bring them back?"

Without missing a beat, he looked me straight in the eyes and said, "You take the fucking Jeep."

"Right," I said, slapping myself on the forehead. "I knew that."

Both John and James were looking at me like I was a mental cripple and waiting for a reply to their original question. "Okay, guys," I said, trying to muster as much dignity as I could. "Go ahead and take the mopeds."

As they were leaving, I knew for a fact that at that moment, I was the dumbest man on the planet. I held this title for many years, but I was finally forced to relinquish it during the 2016 Republican Presidential Debates.

After John and James returned from their moped ride, they thanked us and said how much they appreciated our letting them try them out.

I then asked, "Any chance we could get an invitation to the clambake tonight?"

James Taylor responded by saying, "Uh, no." Off they went with their salt water. Off we went with a lifelong memory.

Lessons Learned

When the kids were growing up, we always had family dinners. Attendance was mandatory, and no TV was allowed. I missed a lot of dinners when I was traveling on business. But I was present whenever possible. Just like families used to do before all of today's distractions came along, we talked and teased and joked and debated.

When I was home during the school year, I would pose a question to each of the children sometime during dinner. "Katie," I would ask, "what did you learn in school today?"

The kids would often try to get away with answering "Nothing." But then I would grill them on why they bothered to get up that morning, why they bothered going all the way to school, and had they ever considered dropping out since there didn't appear to be much purpose to being there.

Once I had asked one of them the daily question, the others knew what was coming and had time to prepare. Their answers usually proved to be very good conversation starters and would often lead to some great discussions about a variety of topics.

For example, I would ask Joseph, "So, Joe, what did you learn in school today?"

He might reply, "I learned that water can take the form of a solid, a liquid, or a gas, depending on its temperature."

"Good," I might respond. "What is solid water called?"

"Ice."

"Right! And do you know what ice does that no other substance on earth does?"

"No clue."

"It floats. Every other substance on earth gets heavier when it freezes except water. It gets lighter when it freezes, and therefore, it floats."

"Big deal," all three of the children would whine.

"It turns out that it is a big deal, a very big deal. What would happen if ice didn't float?" I would ask.

Then there would be a lot of guessing and reasoning and back and forth on the question. After a while, I might start giving them hints.

"If ice were heavier than water, where would it sit in your water glass?" I would ask.

"On the bottom," one of the kids would eventually say.

"Bingo! And what if the ice were in a lake?"

"It would sink to the bottom," another would answer.

"And then what would happen to the fish?"

After thinking for a minute, one of them would come up with the answer: "The ice would trap them all on the bottom, and they would die."

"Very good," I would respond. "Now just out of curiosity, does this make any of you think that there must be a God? Water is the only substance on the planet that gets lighter when it freezes. And if that weren't the case, there would be no fish. It's almost like God got to that point in his creation of the earth and said, 'Oops—that'll never work. Well, I know how I can fix it. I'll just make the ice float instead of sink. Problem solved.'"

These were great conversations, and there was often a lesson to be learned. I also think that these discussions did a lot to bring our family closer together. Of course, food fights, which I frequently declared, went a long way too.

Like all families, ours was forever learning lessons—sometimes the easy way, but usually the hard way. Katie learned an important lesson all on her own. When she was a junior in high school, she decided she wanted to throw a party for a group of extended friends, maybe thirty or forty people. We lived in a big house in Greenwich, Connecticut, at the time, and there was a huge, 800-square-foot playroom on the third floor. When the house was built in 1855, and for many years thereafter, this room was said to have been the ballroom. Anyway, space for the party was not an issue.

We told Katie that she was welcome to have a party and that she could invite whomever she chose, but there would be three firm rules: (1) no drugs, (2) no alcohol, and (3) no closed bedroom doors. Otherwise, have a great time.

Katie organized her party, invited her friends and their friends, and got ready for the big night. On the Saturday of the party, she iced down the soda, put together sandwich platters, set out snacks, cued up the music, and otherwise got ready to go.

About seven thirty that evening, folks started showing up. By eight o'clock, there were about forty people at the party. By nine o'clock, there were maybe sixty people. At that point, I quit counting. Bonita and I watched TV in the living room, far removed from the party, but we did do a walk-through every hour or so just to be sure that there were no rule violations.

At about eleven thirty, the party started winding down. Katie and her close friends had everything cleaned up and back to normal by midnight. After her friends had departed, Katie joined us in the living room.

"Never again," she announced.

"What happened?" we asked.

"I spent the entire evening enforcing the rules," she said. "My friends got the message and didn't bring any alcohol. But some of their friends did. Then the word got out that I was having a party, and a bunch of other people started showing up. I'd estimate that at one point, there were over eighty people here. I didn't know half of them. And almost all of them brought beer."

"I spent the most of the night patrolling inside and outside the house, confiscating beer. At least I didn't see any drugs and the bedroom doors stayed open throughout the party. But the beer patrol wasn't any fun. This was supposed to be a party, not a policing action. At one point, I saw that three people had crawled out of my bedroom window and were sitting on the roof drinking beer. Whew! I'm worn out."

"We're proud of you, Katie," Bonita said. "You took the rules seriously and did the best you could in a situation that got a bit out of hand. Nice job. You can have another party whenever you want."

"Never again," Katie reaffirmed. "Or at least not for another five years."

Lesson Learned: Don't throw a big party until all the guests can legally drink.

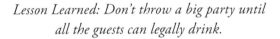

Anna taught me a life-changing lesson that has stayed with me to this day. In 1995, Anna was thirteen. One day Bonita got tied up with something and didn't get started on dinner until it was too late. When I arrived home from the office, she asked me if I minded having McDonald's for dinner. I said not only was that fine, but that I'd go get it.

"Who wants to go to Mickey Ds with Dad?" I asked the kids.

"I do," said Anna, and off we went.

When we got to McDonald's, we went inside to order. For the five of us, the order was probably eight sandwiches and five french fries. A nice young lady at the counter took our order and said, "That will take a few minutes, sir."

As we waited, my gaze drifted over to the french fry machine. I knew the employees were hard at work in the back preparing our sandwiches. But there was nothing happening at the french fry machine. I could see what was going to happen: When our server finally picked up our sandwiches, she would turn to get the fries and discover that she had to cook more. She would then say, "It'll just be a minute on the fries, sir."

My blood pressure started going up, my neck started to turn red, and I was just about to start yelling. That's when Anna turned to me and said, "Dad, did you ever think that if everybody was as smart as you, there wouldn't be anybody to work at McDonald's?"

Talk about pulling me up short. I immediately calmed down and thought about what Anna had just said. She was right. It wasn't the server's fault that she wasn't blessed with a sharp mind or a good memory. This girl was doing the best she could.

I actually said "no problem" when she handed us the bag of sandwiches and said, as I knew she would, "It'll just be another minute on the fries."

Anna's observation really changed my life. To this day, whenever I get faced with crummy service or dumb clerks or forgetful waiters, I am reminded of Anna's question. It seems to me that most people on the planet are generally trying to do the best that they can, given what God gave them to work with. This was the lesson that Anna taught me.

Lesson Learned: Never criticize the performance of a service worker unless you would be willing to take their job.

—••••————•————•••—

Joseph taught us yet another valuable lesson. As I remember, he was about thirteen years old. I was sitting on the back porch one Saturday working the *New York Times* crossword puzzle. I've worked the *Times* crossword puzzle every day for forty years. It has become a ritual.

After a time, Bonita came out and joined me. "You have got to fix your son," she declared.

"What did he do?" I asked.

"He's been going on to porn sites on the computer."

"How do you know?"

"I checked the history file."

"The computer actually has a history file?" I asked. "I never knew."

"What are the sites? And how do you know that they're porn?" I continued.

"There were a bunch of them, with names like 'Busty Babes' and 'Susie Bares All.'"

"Well at least they don't seem to be sick or perverted," I offered, trying to cut Joe some slack.

"Fix him!" she demanded. "Now! He's your son, and this behavior is not appropriate for a thirteen-year-old young man. It's your job to fix it."

I found Joseph in his bedroom and sat down for one of those father-son talks.

"Joe," I said, "your mother claims she found evidence that you've been checking out some online porn websites. Is that true?"

"Yeah, it's true," he answered. "What did she do, check the history file?"

"I guess so," I replied. "But to be honest, until five minutes ago, I didn't even know that there was such a thing as a history file. Look, Joe, I understand that you have reached an age where you are curious about sex and curious about women's bodies, and there is nothing wrong with that. It's nothing to be embarrassed about. It's natural and normal. But we can't have your mother freaking out. Do you understand?"

"Yeah, Dad," he said. "I get it."

"Great," I said. "Now when I was your age, I used to hide a *Playboy* magazine under my mattress. And I never got caught. Do you want me to get you a copy of *Playboy* and show you how to hide it?"

"No thanks, Dad," he replied. "From now on, I'll just delete the history file."

Lesson Learned: Always delete the history file after viewing porn.

Mud Dive

G ail and Gloria Hamilton are our lifelong friends. In fact, they are really lifelong family. Our children view Gloria somewhere between a crazy aunt and a loving confidant. They view Gail as a wise and caring counselor, like a patient and understanding grandfather. They have been part of our lives since 1975, five years before our oldest child was born.

And by part of our lives, I mean a big part of our lives. Bonita and I have traveled the world with Gail and Gloria. The four of us have been to New England, Las Vegas, Florida, and Europe. They visited us probably fifty times between Cleveland, Atlanta, Greenwich, and Naples. And we have frequently visited them at their home in Bellefontaine, Ohio, Bonita's hometown. We've spent a lot of time together over the years, good times all.

When we lived in Atlanta and Greenwich, they would come for a week at Christmas every other year. For years, Gail used to come to Connecticut by himself every August for a week, and he and I would go to five or six New York Yankee games. Given the frequency of his visits, he knew lots of people at Yankee Stadium. And he was known by all of them as Mr. Mayor, in part because he was the spitting image of David Dinkins, the mayor of New York from 1990 to 1993, and in part because Gail had served as mayor of his hometown, Bellefontaine, Ohio, from 1996 to 2000.

His mayoral election in 1995 was a pretty amazing feat. In 2000, Bellefontaine, Ohio—the county seat of Logan County, Ohio—was

96 percent white and less than 2 percent African American. And it is very conservative, with about 66 percent of voters registered as Republicans. Gail was an African American Democrat. But he staged a major upset and became Bellefontaine's first black mayor.

The interesting thing about our relationship with Gail and Gloria is not that they are an interracial couple. When they got married in 1952, it was a very difficult thing to do; but by the time we became friends, it was not such an uncommon occurrence. No, the surprise is our age differences. As of this writing Bonita is sixty-two, and I am sixty-seven; Gail is ninety, and Gloria is ninety-two. That's a pretty big age gap, but for whatever reason, our friendship just clicked. We have fun together. We respect one another. We love one another. We cherish any time that we can spend together. We have definitely had some good times, and we have definitely let them roll. Gail and Gloria are eternally young. Either that, or Bonita and I are eternally old.

One of our more memorable evenings took place in London, England, in October 2000. It had always been my goal to retire at age fifty. I don't think that God put us on the earth to work our buns off for fifty years and then die two years after retiring. That math just always seemed wrong to me. I've heard it said that "It's better to be lucky than good." I hope that I was good; but I know that I was lucky.

Young & Rubicam bought our management consulting firm in 1997, and while we didn't get a lot of cash, we did get a lot of stock options. From 1997 to 2000, I served as the chief financial officer of Burson-Marsteller. B-M was the largest subsidiary of the huge advertising agency Y&R.

I was part of the team that took Y&R public in 1998, and my stock options suddenly became much more valuable. But I hit the jackpot when Y&R sold to the WPP Group, another big advertising conglomerate, for almost $5 billion in May of 2000. That made my options worth a lot of money. I remember coming home and telling Bonita, "If you don't want to make any major changes to our lifestyle, we've got enough money to retire." The sale closed on October 2, and I retired the next day, six days shy of my fifty-first birthday.

Shortly thereafter, Bonita and I decided to go to Europe for two weeks to celebrate, and we invited our dear friends Gail and Gloria to join us. They readily agreed. We decided that this was going to be a once-in-a-lifetime celebration. We planned to spend one night gambling, so I took along $10,000 with complete indifference as to whether I won money or lost my entire stake. I have always been cautious when I have gambled. I never wanted to get liquored up, do something really dumb, and lose a lot of money.

But for just one night, I wanted to be stupid and crazy and throw caution to the wind. If I lost a lot of money in the process, so what! I meant to celebrate, blow off steam, and have a hell of a lot of fun with my wife and friends. The money was meant to fund all four of us for a night at the Ritz Club, my casino of choice in London. And that it did.

We were all dressed to the nines. When we arrived, we went straight to the bar for some drinks. Then we moved on into the dining room for dinner. At that time, the food at the Ritz Club was probably the best in London. As I recall, Gail and I requested a special order of lobster thermidor, which the chef prepared to perfection. Dessert, coffee, a digestif, and a nice cigar rounded out a perfect dinner. The ladies skipped the cigars.

We then adjourned to the gambling floor for some serious fun. I am a die-hard blackjack fan, as is Bonita. But blackjack is not really crazy or fun or socially interactive in the way that roulette is. So we headed for the roulette tables. I took out several thousand dollars to get us started and passed around a bunch of £25 and £100 chips to Bonita, Gail, and Gloria.

I said to Gail that we needed a strategy for the evening. In roulette, the odds don't change on any number on any spin, but I wanted something to cheer for and something to use as a momentum-builder. I suggested that we bet on the uniform numbers of famous New York Yankee players. Gail agreed. Derek Jeter (2), Babe Ruth (3), Lou Gehrig (4), Joe DiMaggio (5), Mickey Mantle (7), Yogi Berra (8), Whitey Ford (16), and Don "Donnie Baseball" Mattingly (23) formed our core betting options.

One of us would put £100 on number 23, and while the wheel was spinning would shout, "Come on, Donnie! We need you, Donnie!" The other would put £50 on number 5 and would shout, "Come on, Joe D.! You can do it, Joe D.!"

In roulette, you can bet on any number from one to thirty-six or zero or double zero, and if you win, you get paid off at 35–1, meaning your £100 bet just turned into £3500. And we were playing four or five or six numbers on each spin.

"Come on, Yogi! Come on, Mickey!"

"Come on, Derek! Get 'er done, Lou!"

"Come on, Whitey! You're the man, Whitey!"

And the money started coming in. We hit some hot streaks. We won some crazy bets. We were beginning to feel invincible. Our Yankee heroes were getting it done for us yet again.

What was really fun to watch was the building excitement around the table. Bonita and Gloria played for a while but then were just as happy to watch Gail and me and the several other players who had joined the table since we had started. Two of the other players were older, white-haired, dignified British gentlemen who gambled silently for some time after they first sat down. But then, little by little, they started to get into the action. Before long, they were shouting:

"Come on, Derek!"

"Let's go, Donnie Baseball!"

We had told them who we were cheering for and why, and even though they had no idea who Derek Jeter or Don Mattingly were, they were rooting for them. And they were rooting louder by the minute.

"Come on, Babe!"

"Come on, Yogi!"

Somehow, these proper British gentlemen were able to get into the action and cheer for players like they were in a rowdy bar in the Bronx. Yet they were still able to maintain their class and their dignity. I think that it might have been their high-pitched, tittery laughs.

And we all just kept on winning. I had gone into the evening willing, even expecting, to lose $10,000. However, try as we might, when we left the casino a little after midnight, I had $16,000 in my pocket. What a night!

Our most memorable story with Gail and Gloria took place on Bonita's and my third date. She and I worked together at a manufacturing plant in Bellefontaine, Ohio, where I was the production control manager. Bonita was a music teacher in real life, but she worked as a fill-in at the plant during the summer. That summer she was filling in for my secretary, who was out on an extended pregnancy leave.

I was recently divorced but was not yet ready to start dating again. Plus I had always made it a practice to avoid dating people from work, particularly subordinates. And our first date wasn't really a date until we looked back on it.

It was a Friday night, and I was preparing for a major presentation to be given to the company CEO and his staff on Monday morning. I needed Bonita to stay late and help me. We finished at about seven thirty, and it dawned on me that I had totally messed up her Friday night.

"I'm sorry," I said. "I hope that you didn't have plans."

"No," she said. "I wasn't doing anything tonight anyway—just catching up on some reading."

"Well, it's getting late. Would you like to get some dinner?" I asked.

"Sure," she said. "That would be great."

I don't remember where we went for dinner—there weren't a lot of choices in Bellefontaine—but I distinctly remember that I fell in love midway through my entrée. We talked and talked and talked and had a delightful time

The next Monday I asked her out on an official date for the upcoming Saturday night, and she said yes. I think that we drove to Columbus so we could eat at a very good restaurant for a change. We were having another great dinner, and I was falling more in love by the minute. We had a far-reaching conversation and discovered that we had a lot of the same interests.

We were most of the way through dinner when I popped the question: "Gail and Gloria and I are leaving next weekend for a week in New England. I don't mean to be too forward, but would you like to go along?"

"I'd love to!" she replied, somewhat to my surprise.

We spent the rest of the evening planning how she could pull this off. Work was no problem since she worked for me. But home was a different story. Bonita still lived with her parents so she could save toward a nest egg for the future. This was 1976, and her parents were very conservative; and they weren't too sure about me since I had been married before. We had to do this on the QT.

After planning her alibi and lining up her coconspirator, Bonita told her folks that she would be spending a week in Dayton with her roommate from college. She drove her car to my house, transferred her luggage to my car, and put her car in my garage so that no one would see it during the week.

We picked up Gail and Gloria, and off we went to New England. There we saw all the sights: Faneuil Hall in Boston; the amusement park at Old Orchard Beach, Maine; the top of Mount Washington in the White Mountains; the state capitol in Montpelier, Vermont; the Vermont Country Store in Weston, Vermont; and much, much more.

We spent one night in Stowe, Vermont, at a cozy, romantic inn. We had a first-class dinner and lots of lively conversation.

As we walked back to our rooms from dinner, Gail began to sing "Moonlight in Vermont." The Mills Brothers were Gail's uncles, and he was blessed with some great pipes. Neither of us will ever forget that night.

The real purpose of the trip was to attend the Craftsbury Fiddler's Contest in Craftsbury, Vermont. Craftsbury is in the northernmost region of Vermont, about thirty-five miles south of Canada.

I remember that late on Friday afternoon, we were in our hotel room, and I was facing Bonita with my back to the television. Many of the television channels were French-speaking stations from Quebec. I heard a man saying something melodic and transfixing in French, and I put my arms around Bonita.

"Isn't that romantic?" I said.

Bonita burst out laughing. I quickly pulled away and turned around only to see a bicycle commercial on television. Only the French can make a bicycle commercial sound seductive. Ooh Lah Lah!

The next morning, we headed for the festival. The Craftsbury Fiddler's Contest was, at that time, an annual event. It was begun in 1962, and I believe that it lasted into the 1980s. It was held outside of town on a farm, sort of like Yasgur's farm for Woodstock. There was a big field with a stage at one end. Fiddle players would come in from all over the country to compete in the contest.

I estimate that there were at least fifty thousand people in attendance and maybe thirty fiddle performers when we were there in 1976. Unfortunately, it had rained for two days prior to the contest and was pouring rain on the day of it. We had stopped in town and bought rain gear. But with that amount of rain, you couldn't stay dry. Plus the mud was ankle deep.

The contest was amazing, and the music was all we had hoped it would be: bluegrass and Virginia reels, down-home country, duos, singles, and trios, all with superb fiddle playing. Some of the groups offered world-class music. Others were more laid back and comical. One fiddler stood in a bathtub while he played, and in the middle of his performance, he shouted out: "I ain't here to compete! I'm here to entertain all of you fine people!" We were having some good times, and we were letting them roll.

And then, panic! Remember that Bonita and I were on a clandestine mission here. Her parents thought she was with her college roommate, Susie, in Dayton. And what do I see out of the corner of my eye? An NBC News reporter and his cameraman, and they were coming our way.

Everyone around us was screaming and waving and jumping, trying to get the cameraman's attention. I had visions of Bonita's folks sitting quietly on the sofa watching the Evening News that night, when who should appear on the screen, live from Craftsbury, Vermont, but their daughter and this interloper jerk whom she had just gone out with once.

I yelled to Bonita and pointed out the NBC guys. She must have had the same thought as I'd had, because the next thing you know, we both had taken a dive straight to the ground. Make that straight into the ankle-deep mud. I could feel the mud oozing up through my clothes. We were covered from top to bottom.

After that maneuver, we were pretty much unrecognizable. Even if we had been on TV, no one would have guessed that it was us. So we stood back up and joined in the fun.

It was a great day of live music performed by some outstanding musicians, a great day of hanging out with dear friends, and a great day of playing in the rain. Bonita even got a T-shirt out of the deal, but she had to be careful where she wore it, as we were never supposed to have been there.

To this day, we contend that during the fifteenth annual Craftsbury Fiddler's Contest, we performed the first and only Craftsbury Mud Dive.

Let's Eat!

Mealtime has always been special at the Krauss house. When the children were growing up, we had family dinners every night. Mealtime was a time to talk, a time to catch up on the day's events, a time for teasing, a time for the kids to share their stories. I have always believed that family meals may be the most important part of successful parenting.

They are also a time for some real yuks and some lasting memories. Katie must have been about fourteen when she announced during a family dinner that she was going to dye her hair purple.

"That's great!" Bonita said.

"Oh boy," I added, "I can't wait. When are you going to do it?"

Katie was astonished. "You mean neither of you guys care if I dye my hair bright purple? I was sure that you would be upset."

"Katie," I explained, "I work really hard and really long hours. My job is serious and stressful. When I get home at night, I'm out of gas. But the thought of sitting down to dinner with you and your purple hair is really refreshing. Think of the laughs. Think of the teasing. I'm sure that purple hair will brighten each and every evening."

Katie was stunned and speechless.

"Anna," Bonita asked, "have you ever thought about dyeing your hair? Blue would be striking."

Obviously, Katie was trying to push some buttons, push some boundaries, and lay claim to her own independence. She was sure that we would object. But the whole exercise lost its purpose once we didn't fight it. Plus, I'm sure that she could imagine the teasing that purple hair would get from the rest of the family. Katie kept her blonde hair, and the subject never came up again.

I have always liked to cook. When I was younger, I was in the Boy Scouts and was part of a troop that went camping at least one weekend a month. I got to be pretty good at cooking over an open fire. My specialty was meat loaf. Do you know that if you build a big fire and keep adding wood until you have a bed of coals that is maybe six or eight inches deep, the temperature of the embers will be 350°? If you bury a meat loaf wrapped in two layers of aluminum foil in the coals for an hour, it will be perfectly done.

My adventures in cooking have continued throughout my life, although when I was working, I didn't have much time to devote to the kitchen. Still, I would occasionally find time to create and prepare what the children referred to as "experimental food." Some of these attempts were terrific; others fell flat. But the fun was in the trying.

I remember once, when Bonita was out of town for some reason, I got inspired to cook something different for that night's family dinner. We all liked meat loaf, and we all liked Italian sausage. So I decided to combine the two. I used my standard Boy Scout meat loaf recipe. Once it was ready to go, I formed the meat loaf around the Italian sausage. If you looked at a cross section, it would look like a donut with the sausage where the hole belongs.

Into the oven it went. About an hour later, I figured it was done, plated it, and took it to the table. When I made the first crosswise cut, I discovered my mistake: Italian sausage cooks a lot slower than hamburger. The meat loaf was fully cooked, but the sausage was still raw in places.

The children were totally grossed out. Even after I got the sausage fully cooked in the microwave, they could not bring themselves to eat it. But that is the risk you run with experimental food. They tease me about it to this day.

"Hey, Dad," one of them will say. "How about you make dinner tonight? I'm in the mood for some of that meat loaf and Italian sausage. Ha!"

It was only a few months later that I redeemed myself quite nicely. On a random Saturday afternoon, the mood struck me. I said that I would cook experimental food for dinner. Bonita was thrilled. The children were nervous.

The entire family liked Sloppy Joes. We had them maybe once a month. We also liked cheap Wisconsin cheese food, like Velveeta. So I thought why not combine some of the ingredients and make a new sandwich, to be known as a Sloppy Cheese? I developed my own recipe and one fateful Saturday night, I tried it out. It was an instant hit, and it became a regular in the rotation.

Here is the recipe:

Dad's Sloppy Cheese

<u>Ingredients</u>
>   6 slices of bacon
>   1 medium onion
>   1/2 teaspoon salt
>   2 pounds ground round
>   1/2 teaspoon ground black pepper
>   8 ounces Velveeta cheese
>   Sesame seed hamburger buns

<u>Directions</u>
>   – Chop onion into 1/4" pieces.
>   – Cut bacon into 1/2" strips.

- Chop Velveeta into 1" cubes.
- Fry bacon on medium-high until 90% cooked.
- Add chopped onion and cook until golden brown.
- Add ground round to bacon/onion mixture.
- Add salt & pepper & stir frequently until done.
- Add cheese & stir until cheese is fully melted.
- Spoon mixture onto bun.

Makes about eight sandwiches; cooking time about twenty minutes.

But be forewarned: You may want to check with your cardiologist before you try Sloppy Cheese. This baby is a true artery clogger. You can actually feel your blood congealing and slowing down. But believe me, it is worth the price. And if you use moderation, I'm sure that things will be fine. We still have Sloppy Cheese maybe four times a year, as it is now a favorite of all three of our grandchildren. And my blood pressure, cholesterol levels, and EKG results continue to be normal.

We didn't have a lot of rules in our family. What was acceptable behavior was pretty much understood, and the kids did a good job of measuring up. As Bill Murray famously said in *Ghostbusters*, "Actually, it's more of a guideline than a rule."

We did have one rule, which we enforced pretty consistently: "No dessert unless you have cleaned your plate." It always seemed inappropriate to reward the children's failure to eat a good, balanced meal by giving them cake or ice cream. We weren't rigid about how big a serving size they needed to eat to qualify for the goodies, only that they took something and that they finish what they took.

As a result, all three children developed a taste for a variety of foods. They were not picky eaters and were always willing to try something new. When Katie and Anna were maybe six and eight years old, they actually preferred shrimp to pizza. Imagine that!

One Saturday, we were all having lunch at our home in Atlanta. Our kitchen table was surrounded on three sides by a big bay window. Anna was sitting with her back to the main window while the rest of us were facing it and looking out into the backyard.

The fare that day was hot dogs, and everyone had a plate holding one hot dog in a bun. Anna had just finished putting mustard on hers but had yet to pick it up.

"Look, Anna. It's a deer," I shouted as I pointed out the window to her right.

As she turned, I snatched her hot dog and took a bite.

"Where?" she asked, turning back around.

"There," I said pointing again and grabbing another bite of her hot dog.

"I still don't see it."

"Right by the tree," I said as I ate the last bite of her hot dog.

Anna gave up on the deer and turned back around. She looked down and noticed that her hot dog was gone.

Then without missing a beat, she asked, "Can I have dessert?"

You can't make this stuff up.

Applause, Applause

New York is the greatest city on the planet. Over the course of my life, I've been fortunate to travel the world. I've been to some great cities: Toronto, Vancouver, Montreal, London, Paris, Rome, Florence, Oslo, Berlin, Dublin, São Paulo, Mexico City, Tokyo, Singapore, Hong Kong, Seoul, and others. And I've visited most of them on multiple occasions. But as great as these cities are, they don't hold a candle to New York City.

We lived in Greenwich, Connecticut, for fifteen years spanning the 1990s and early 2000s. We were only about a half hour by car from Grand Central Station. It was about the same distance to Little Italy in Manhattan as it was to the real Little Italy on Arthur Avenue in the Bronx as it was to Yankee Stadium and to Lincoln Center and to Carnegie Hall and to Broadway and to some of the best restaurants in the world.

My office was in Greenwich, but even so, someone in the family was in New York City maybe three times a week. I went to fifty to sixty Yankee games every year. Bonita and I went in for dinner at least once every two weeks. We routinely had tickets to Broadway shows, Lincoln Center concerts, and Carnegie Hall recitals.

When they were old enough, the kids would take the train into the city on weekends with their friends just to walk around neighborhoods like Soho and Greenwich Village and take in the sights, the sounds, and the smells.

We took the children to Little Italy in Manhattan for dinner on Sunday maybe twice a month. We had world-class pizza, walked the neighborhood, and then went to Ferrara's for cannoli or gelato before returning home.

Ferrara's opened in 1892 and has been a favored destination of New Yorkers ever since. Here is how their website describes the origin of this family-owned New York landmark:

> New York in the Gay Eighteen Nineties had almost everything, except for a place where an opera lover, after a night of Verdi or Puccini, could relax, play a Neapolitan card game called "Scopa" and drink a cup or two of espresso.
>
> This situation was remedied in 1892 when our great grandfather, Enrico Scoppa and our great grand-uncle, Antonio Ferrara, opera impresario and showman, opened a cafe called Café A. Ferrara. Caruso thought the coffee marvelous but especially loved the cookies and cakes.

Bonita and I both loved New York City even before we lived there. Beginning in 1978, I frequently had to be in NYC on business. Before the children were born, I would stay over on the weekend and Bonita would fly in and join me. Even after the Yard Apes came along, we would try to arrange these weekends away whenever we could.

One place that we visited on many occasions was the Café Carlyle, located in the basement of the Carlyle Hotel on the Upper Eastside. This is a very special place and it is quintessentially New York. From their website:

> The golden age of New York cabaret comes alive each night at Café Carlyle. With an authentic Manhattan

backdrop and a soundtrack that is classic cabaret, Café Carlyle is known for headlining incredible talents; including Sutton Foster, Judy Collins and Woody Allen, who regularly appears to jam with the Eddy Davis New Orleans jazz band. Music has been an essential part of The Carlyle, and it has been on spectacular display at the Café Carlyle since its debut in 1955.

Seating up to 90 for dinner and a performance, the supper club offers a unique intimate space and is highlighted by music-themed wall murals by Marcel Vertès. At Café Carlyle, guests experience and engage in the lost language of elegance and sophistication. As the New York bastion of classic cabaret entertainment, Café Carlyle completes the Manhattan experience.

Before his death in 2005, Bobby Short used to appear at the Carlyle regularly. As I remember, he would do two ninety minute shows each night: one at 9:00 p.m. and the other at 11:00 p.m. He would play the piano and sing the classic songs of Duke Ellington, Cole Porter, Ira Gershwin, and their contemporaries. He had such presence and class and elegance that if you saw him once, you would never forget him.

The Café Carlyle was also a fine restaurant. When I was traveling to New York City on business, I liked nothing better than to work in the office until maybe eight o'clock and then go to the Carlyle for drinks and dinner, sometimes with a colleague and sometimes by myself. Just about the time I was served my main course, Bobby Short would start his nine o'clock show. I would eat my dinner, perhaps enjoy a little dessert, and, for sure, have a couple of after-dinner drinks, all the while listening to Bobby Short play the piano and sing. What a treat.

One night after we had moved to Connecticut, Bonita and I decided to go to the Café Carlyle to see one of our favorite pianists, George Shearing. As I remember, Bobby Short was on vacation and George was filling in for six weeks. As you may know, George Shearing was totally blind, so when he was introduced, he was led to his piano by his bass player, Brian Torff.

The show was terrific. That night he played many of his classics: "The Nearness of You," "Have You Met Miss Jones," and "Blue Prelude" to name three. And it was no surprise when George finished up with his most well-known jazz standard, "Lullaby of Birdland." The crowd leapt to their feet, giving Mr. Shearing the standing ovation that he deserved.

It was another great performance for Mr. Shearing. As he was being lead out of the room by Mr. Torff, a guy in the audience shouted to him, "Outta sight, George!"

Without missing a beat, George turned in his direction and said, "Yeah, at least one of us is."

George was one of the best jazz piano players there ever was. We lost a great one when he died in 2011.

In 1979, my second year at Booz Allen, I was in New York on client business with my colleague Harry Thompson from Chicago. Since we had to be there on Friday of one week and Monday of the next, we both decided to bring our wives in for the weekend. Bonita and Harry's wife, Donna, flew in on Friday afternoon, and the four of us proceeded to have a classic New York weekend. It was two weeks before Christmas, so the city was decked out in fine form.

On Saturday night, we had reservations at the Café Carlyle for the 11:00 p.m. Bobby Short show. We arrived and were seated on the side nearest to the entrance. The place holds only ninety people, so there is not a bad seat to be found. We'd already had dinner, so we ordered a round of drinks and settled in for the show.

About ten minutes before it began, I looked to my right and who did I see coming in the door? It was none other than Howard Cosell, the arrogant, loud-mouthed, rather boorish sportscaster from ABC. This was the peak time for Howard on *Monday Night Football*. He was as famous as he was obnoxious.

The maître d' greeted him by saying, "May I help you, sir?"

"We need a table for two," Howard said in his booming voice. "I'd like one on the right side of the room a little behind the piano."

"Do you have a reservation?" the maître d' asked.

"No, we don't," Howard replied.

"Well, I'm sorry, sir, but we are completely sold out tonight. I don't have anything available," the maître d' explained.

"Do you know who I am?" Howard said loudly and belligerently.

"No, sir," the maître d' said, his voice getting louder too. "I have no idea who you are."

"I am Howard Cosell," he shouted for all to hear.

"I don't care if you're the King of England!" the maître d' shouted back for all to hear. "We have no tables!"

Howard turned abruptly, grabbed his wife by the arm, and headed for the door. As he was leaving, the entire café broke out in rousing applause. It was one of those "only in New York" nights.

Friends

Life is short. Smile while you still have teeth.

Balls

In 1981, I was offered the opportunity to relocate to Booz Allen's office in Atlanta, in order to lead the firm's operations practice in the southeast United States. I said yes immediately. Bonita and I bought a house in Atlanta, sold our house in Cleveland, and moved to the Peach State.

It was tough leaving our family and friends behind in Ohio. Both Bonita and I were born and bred Buckeyes, and except for a two-year stint at graduate school at Carnegie Mellon University in Pittsburgh, I had never lived outside of Ohio. This was Bonita's first out-of-state move.

We slowly but surely made new friends in Atlanta; some from work, some from the neighborhood. But when the holidays approached, we began to get homesick. Then we had the big idea. Why not invite all our friends from the North to a New Year's Eve party at our place? As we thought about it, we realized that no one in their right mind would drive 1200 miles round-trip for a three-hour party. Talk about a nonstarter. So we worked the problem from the other end. How long would a party have to last, and how would we go about persuading people to travel 1200 miles? That first year—yes, this party would continue in one form or another for twenty years—we thought that a four-day party with fun daily activities would get 'er done.

We wrote a thirteen-page invitation that tried to capture the reader's imagination and invited thirty out-of-town friends. Then we invited eight local friends. We ended up with a total of seventeen folks at that first four-day party. Many memories of this party have disappeared into a fog. But I do remember that everyone had a really good time.

After the main event—a five-hour New Year's Eve party with food, booze, music, dance cards, the works—a bunch of us were sitting in our living room. It was about three in the morning, and we had just finished a snack of fried egg sandwiches and Bloody Marys. Bonita's cousin-in-law, Walter Wyse, was sharing a piano bench with my graduate school roommate, Jim Bachman.

Walter was sitting on the far left end of the bench. During a lull in the conversation, Walter looked up and announced to the entire room, "This is the most fun I've ever had in my whole life!" And then he passed out and fell straight off the side of the piano bench.

Jim turned toward him and said, "That man deserves a trophy!"

Thus was born the whole idea of giving out trophies for desirable or despicable or admirable party behaviors. The first award was a large trophy named the Walter Wyse Cup. It was to be given to the one individual who had the most fun and exhibited the most joy over the entire duration of each annual party. And of course, Walter was the first recipient when the awards were first presented on December 31, 1982.

A number of lesser awards were also established to recognize and reinforce various elements of party behavior:

- Ron Comer Trophy for consumption of food and liquor
- Gloria Hamilton Trophy for creativity in party attire
- Magic Feet Award for adept and magical dancing
- Balls Award for the most outrageous act

These awards were presented every year in a formal ceremony presided over by yours truly: the self-declared Imperial Potentate of New Year's Eve.

The most coveted award was the Walter Wyse Cup. But the most interesting and anticipated honor every year was the Balls Award for the most outrageous act.

Two of these acts stand out in my memory. The first took place in 1986. My cousin Bill Krauss and I are as close as brothers. And in the eighties, Bill always sported a full beard. By full, I mean really full: part man, part bear.

At eleven forty-five, Bill slipped away from the party. At midnight, he quietly slipped back in. Cousin Bill had shaved off his beard and had slicked back his hair.

He started out looking like a bearded biker:

He ended up looking like a metrosexual:

The hysterical part was that nobody noticed Bill's transformation because nobody recognized him. It was at least fifteen minutes later when Gail Hamilton, who was standing right next to him, somewhat incredulously said, "Bill?" The word then traveled quickly. Cousin Billy had balls.

As cool as Bill's stunt was, my favorite Balls Award winners were Bill and Nona Greene. In 1989, they ignored the suggested party attire of elegant tops and casual bottoms, and they instead came dressed in full formal dress: tuxedo, silk shirt, tie and cummerbund, and black dress shoes for Bill; long gown, high heels, and killer jewelry for Nona. They, too, quietly slipped out at eleven forty-five. When they returned twenty minutes later, they had both swapped clothes. Nona had on Bill's entire tuxedoed outfit, including his socks and shoes; and Bill had on Nona's gown, jewelry, and, most impressively, her high heels.

We didn't check out their underwear, but Bill and Nona never did anything half way. Plus, it was sort of scary because they both seemed to be enjoying themselves way too much. What a sight they made. Balls!

Sunset

Bonita and I have been going to Naples, Florida, for thirty-five years. For fifteen years, we stayed at the Edgewater Beach Hotel, a first-class resort right on the Gulf of Mexico. We always had a two-bedroom suite overlooking the water, and we really took advantage of all the amenities. The pool and the beach and the pool bar were obvious spots when the typical weather was 82° and sunny. But in the good old days, they also had steel drum musicians almost every day and crab races for the kids once a week. This really was a slice of paradise.

Twenty years ago, we bought a three-bedroom condominium at the Diplomat, right next door to the Edgewater Beach. This was a bigger, better slice of paradise. Our condo is directly on the beach. If I had to, I could jump from our second-floor lanai into the swimming pool. And best of all, there are only twenty-seven condos, and all the owners are great folks.

We regularly have parties—Super Bowl parties, birthday parties, Sunday night pizza parties, and cocktail parties—and everyone in residence is always invited. Most usually show up. Many of the owners and renters have formed lifelong friendships that go way beyond the Diplomat.

The owners and the returning renters are a close-knit group. The age range spans maybe fifty years. There are over-the-top Republicans and wacko liberal Democrats. There are retired folks and those who still work. Most have children and grandchildren who frequently visit; we've known most of them since they were born.

One ritual that has been going on for years is to assemble around the pool with cocktails and appetizers every night at sunset, weather permitting. Usually, about three or four nights a week, there will be a group down for sunset. Sometimes it's only six people. Other times there might be thirty. Everyone brings their own beverage, and many folks bring appetizers for all to share.

The first night that I met Galen Barnes was memorable. Galen is the former chief operating officer of Nationwide Insurance. He held this job for many years and served on Nationwide's board of directors. He was, and still is, a big deal. But he is also very humble and self-effacing. When I met him, I had heard that he used to have a big job at Nationwide, but I didn't know any more information than that.

So I asked him, "I hear you worked at Nationwide. What did you do there?"

"I came up through the actuarial ranks," he answered, demonstrating his humble nature.

Actuaries are the math whizzes that calculate all the mortality tables and risk factors that insurance companies use in setting their rates. Some might call them nerds. I personally call them very smart.

Anyway, before I could push him on what kind of big job he'd had, Galen said, "Kurt, do you know the difference between an introverted and an extroverted actuary?"

"No idea," I replied.

"An extroverted actuary looks at the other guy's shoes."

This then led to an extended discussion of extroverts and introverts, which led to a discussion of converts, which led to a discussion of perverts, which led to a discussion of the Kentucky basketball team. You get the idea.

Galen was also the subject of an ongoing sunset saga. It involved a widow named Mona Carroll. She had rented one of the condos for the season for the previous three or four years. Mona was a regular at sunset and always brought some scrumptious appetizers. She also was very fond of men and seemingly had a thing for insurance men.

Mona was not only a widow—she was a four-time widow. She went through husbands the way many women go through purses. And two of her dear departed husbands had worked in insurance: one as a salesman, the other as an executive. Guess which one came first.

As I said, Mona was fond of men. She was very solicitous of all the guys: Carl, Bob, Larry, Michael, Ed, Charlie, me. But she paid extra special attention to Galen.

"Can I get you some pâté, Galen?"

"Why thank you, Mona."

"It's my pleasure, Galen."

I guess none of us should have been surprised. After all, Galen was a former insurance company executive, and a big-time insurance executive at that.

The other thing about Mona was that she liked her booze. By the end of our sunset parties, which lasted only maybe ninety minutes, Mona was usually pretty well-oiled.

There were a few occasions when, after sunset, Galen would find himself alone on the elevator with Mona. We all conjectured that the combination of the sun and the liquor and an insurance man would prove powerful, perhaps irresistible, for Mona. Galen would never come right out and say what happened. But he did say that those elevator rides made him "very uncomfortable."

As Paul Harvey used to say: "And now for the rest of the story." Two years later, Mona started dating and eventually married husband number five, Jerry Gold. You guessed it. Jerry was the former CEO of a major insurance company.

One night at sunset, Bob Woolery and Ann Aldridge had some friends from Kentucky visiting them. From Bob, I've learned that in Kentucky, everyone knows everyone: governors, coaches, executives, lawyers, PR men, railroaders, you name it. So I've gotten used to the diversity of his friends and neighbors. Bob introduced this couple as Jim and Susan, and he claimed that Jim was a big University of Kentucky fan. That was no surprise, as virtually all of Bob and Ann's friends are big UK fans.

As it often did, the conversation worked its way around to Kentucky sports, and specifically to football. As we drank, I began to offer my thoughts about UK's football program.

"Jim," I started, "I've seen Kentucky play more than a few times. In fact, I've seen a couple of games live in Lexington with Bob. I don't think that they are too far away from being nationally competitive. Their first teams seem to generally be pretty solid. They are rarely dominated in the first half of any game. In my view, the problem is with the second and third teams. They are inferior to those of their opponents. And when the first team needs a rest, their replacements get blown away."

"Your wrong," countered Jim. "We are not nationally competitive in football, and that's because recruiting is next to impossible. Kentucky's population is only four million, and the best high school athletes tend to focus on basketball. Ohio is just the opposite: twelve million people and a passion for football. We just can't compete."

"That's not how I see it," I continued. "Ohio State's first and second teams are pretty much interchangeable during a game. But who would want to be the backup tackle for UK?"

"Kurt," my good friend Bob interrupted. "I didn't mention it earlier, but Jim used to be the athletic director at the University of Kentucky."

"Well, in that case," I said, "I'll shut my mouth."

One of the ongoing hot topics at sunset was green flashes. According to Wikipedia,

> Green flashes are optical phenomena that sometimes occur right after sunset or right before sunrise. When the conditions are right, a green spot is visible above the upper rim of the disk of the sun. The green appearance usually lasts for no more than a second or two. Green flashes occur because the atmosphere can cause the light from the sun to separate out into different colors.

There was a ceaseless debate, at times heated and passionate, about the existence of green flashes. They are very rare events, and so proof is difficult to come by. We would often go two or three years without anyone claiming to have seen a green flash.

The debates went on all the time. One camp swore that they had seen green flashes and that they surely existed. Some produced supposed pictures, although they were always a bit suspect.

The other side said that they had been watching Florida sunsets for thirty years and had never seen a green flash. They claimed that it was all a hoax played on unsuspecting newcomers and tourists.

I can honestly attest that I have personally seen three green flashes over the years. But I also must admit that I have not seen one since I quit drinking three years ago. Skol!

Debbie

You've already heard about our annual New Year's Eve parties. Here is another treasured memory. As I said, we began these events in 1981. Ten years later, the party was held from December 27, 1990, through January 2, 1991. We invited one hundred and thirty-four friends—and seventy-five showed up—for seven days.

By 1990, the number of officially sanctioned party events had also grown in number and popularity. There was the Early Bird Arrival Dinner, the Arrival Dinner, the Oyster Fest, Shrimp Feast & Pig Out, the Planning Committee Meeting, the Party, Bill Greene's Omelets, the Farewell Dinner, and the Last Hurrah. As of January 1, 1991, ninety-four souls had attended one or more of these parties, and four folks had perfect attendance records. These were truly parties to end all parties. The annual Krauss House New Year's Party lasted for twenty-five years. Great fun! Great friends! Great memories! Let the good times roll!

Speaking of memories, here is perhaps my favorite. I think it occurred in 1986. Monday, December 29, was officially designated as Arrival Day. And that was when the boys went grocery shopping for the week. Obviously, thorough grocery lists were prepared in advance, as we needed to get enough food to feed up to seventy people for five or six days. Usually four guys would join me at a nearby Kroger store, and each would be assigned a cart. I would then direct them:

"Gail, go get twenty-eight half gallons of Tropicana orange juice—no pulp."

"Jim, we need fifteen dozen eggs."

"Ron, find me twenty pounds of Jimmy Dean's pork sausage, and not that sage crap that you got last year."

The whole process took maybe forty-five minutes, and we'd end up with six or seven fully loaded carts. We would then proceed to an available cashier, where upon I would tell the cashier, "Put them all together."

After we took the groceries home, we'd head to the Rusty Nail Tavern, purveyor of the best chicken wings in town. We'd load up on hot wings and beer until three o'clock, at which point we were very happy guys who were feeling no pain. Then we would hurry home for a midafternoon nap.

On this particular day, as we were heading down Roswell Road on our return home, we passed a gas station. In the corner of the station lot, we saw a white car with the trunk open. There were a number of purses and scarves on display in and around the trunk. And there was a very attractive blond standing next to the car.

I did a quick right turn into the gas station and drove up to the apparent "store on wheels." Five well-oiled guys piled out of the car to check out the merchandise. The nice-looking lady introduced herself as Debbie Stovich and told us that this was our lucky day. She said that she had recently come into the possession of some authentic Hermes scarves, some real Louis Vuitton handbags, and a few Rolex Presidential watches and that she was selling them at a huge discount.

My cousin Bill and I took over the negotiations. We asked Debbie about the Rolex watches, and she assured us of their authenticity. We looked at them closely, and they seemed pretty real to us.

So we asked Debbie, "How much?"

"Twenty-five dollars each," she replied.

"What if we buy two?"

"Two for forty dollars."

"Sold!" we proclaimed.

Imagine, we each got an authentic $10,000 Rolex Presidential for only $20. How lucky can two guys get?

We donned our new watches and headed for home. When we arrived, all the women were gathered in the kitchen.

Bill's wife, Connie, said, "So Billie Boy, what's up with the new watch?"

I jumped in to try to save Bill from himself. "Connie," I said, "after the grocery shopping, we decided to go to Phipps Plaza and try a new place that was reported to have great hot wings. As we were leaving the wing joint, we walked past a jewelry store and noticed a sign in the window that said 'Rolex Watch Sale.' So we went inside to check it out. Sure enough, all of the Rolexes were on sale for 40 percent off. Now as you know, both Bill and I have always coveted the Rolex Presidential, although the $10,000 price tag was always a showstopper. But with 40 percent off, we thought that this might be our best chance to own one. So we each bought a gold Presidential."

Connie went off: "You did what? You go out and get all liquored up and then go buy a $6,000 watch? Are you nuts?"

Then Bonita decided to weigh in: "You're just going to have to take them back. Neither of you can afford a $6,000 watch."

"Sorry," I said. "We were told that all sale merchandise purchases were final. No returns."

The shit was just about to hit the proverbial fan when Cousin Bill said, "Hold on a minute. I seem to have a problem with my new Rolex. It looks like the second hand is getting stuck on the diamond in the two o'clock position. It keeps hitting it and bouncing back. It can't get past the diamond."

He took his Rolex and started banging it on the kitchen counter. Bam! Bam! Bam! He then picked the watch up and looked at it. "There, that seemed to fix it," he said.

By that time all the guys were laughing so hard that they were crying. And Connie K., Connie C., Bonita, Alicia, and Gloria had finally figured it out. They were pissed off for only a couple of hours.

I often wonder what became of Debbie. I keep hoping that I'll run into her. Debbie had the goods.

The Commish Letter

I 've hung out at the pool bar at the Edgewater Beach Hotel in Naples, Florida, for over thirty years. And I've become friends with every bartender that has ever worked there since 1982. In the spring of 2009, two of my bartender buddies, Sammy and Greg, and I talked about starting a Suicide League for the upcoming NFL season. If you're not familiar with Suicide Leagues, here is a primer from suicideleague.com, the site which manages our league:

> What is a Suicide League you ask? Some people refer it as survivor, elimination or knock out pool. Each week you pick one NFL team to win their game. If that team wins you move on to the next week. But you cannot pick that same team for the rest of the regular season. If the team you picked loses you are out of the pool for the rest of the season.

The problem with a true Suicide League is that given the frequency of weekly upsets in the NFL, you statistically need over a thousand players to have a shot of making it all the way through the season with even one player left standing.

We play a modified version of a true Suicide League, called a Points League. You still pick one team each week of the NFL season, and you can pick a given team only once per year. But you stay in the competition for the whole year. In any week, if your pick wins, you win the number of points that they won by. If they lose, you lose the number of points that they lost by. Craziness then ensues.

We have always charged a $50 entry fee, and last year we had eighty players. That is a $4000 pot. At the end of the year, the team with the most points wins 80 percent of the pot. Last year that was $3200. The person who scores the fewest points wins the remaining 20 percent, $800 last year.

I am the commissioner of our league, appropriately named PARADISE, given that it was born in Naples, Florida. Every week, I write a Commish Letter to all the team owners/players bringing them up to date on the standings in the league. Other material sometimes finds its way into these weekly letters. God knows why, but it does.

These communiqués are a blast to write. I usually go off on a rant or two. The league has grown to the point that I personally know only half of the owners. But I still tease the hell out of all of them and their dumbass picks.

The highlight of each letter is an observation, question, story, or word of the week. Here are some of The Commish's favorites:

How can someone "draw a blank"?

"Honey, does this dress make me look fat?" "Why do you ask? Does this shirt make me look stupid?"

Do cannibals not eat clowns because they taste funny?

Why do they call the place where you punch your time card a "time" clock? Aren't all clocks "time" clocks?

The world would be a better place to live if stupidity was painful.

I didn't make it to the gym today. That makes five years in a row.

Why do they report power outages on TV?

I don't like making plans for the day because then the word "premeditated" gets thrown around in the courtroom.

It's only when you see a mosquito land on your testicles that you realize that there is always a way to solve problems without resorting to violence.

The world would be a better place to live if instead of a beer belly, you'd get beer biceps.

Did you hear about the fellow whose entire left side was cut off? He's all right now.

Can race officials ban wheelchair athletes from competition if they test positive for WD40?

On average, an American man will have sex two or three times a week; whereas, a Japanese man will have sex only one or two times a year. This is very upsetting news to me. I had no idea I was Japanese.

You're not really drunk unless you have to hold on to the grass to keep from falling off of the earth.

I always wondered what the job application is like at Hooters. Do they just give you a bra and say, "Here, fill this out"?

The location of your mailbox shows how far you can walk in a robe, before you start looking like a mental patient.

This I Do Declare!
Do Dah, Do Dah, Oh Do Dah Day

The Commish

Senator Sam

H ere's another story about our annual New Year's Eve party. As I said before, we began these events in 1981, shortly after we moved to Atlanta. We were feeling a bit homesick and used a multiday party to entice our closest friends and family to visit us. We continued to host these annual events for twenty-five years.

There was a lot of alcohol consumed at these parties. I know that you may find that hard to believe. But trust me, it is true. The Ron Comer Trophy, which Mr. Comer himself won from 1981 to 1984, celebrated the total consumption of food and liquor during the entire party. And there was no lack of competition.

By 1983, it had become clear that an extraordinary amount of time was being wasted by everyone trying to describe to others just how inebriated they had become or intended to become at various party events.

Therefore, the Planning Committee proposed a simple hierarchy of the ten stages of common drunkenness. This was approved by me, the Imperial Potentate of New Year's Eve, on January 1, 1984.

The Ten Official Stages of Drunkenness

1. Loose & Agile
2. Witty & Charming
3. Smart & Articulate
4. Smooth & Sophisticated
5. Rich & Powerful
6. Philosophical
7. Confused & Afraid
8. Morose & Despondent
9. Invisible
10. Bulletproof

Most people hovered between levels 4 and 6 during most party events. But there were exceptions. Jim Farley was unanimously declared to be at level 9—"Invisible"—during a three-hour period on the evening of December 31, 1989.

Many people couldn't understand how we were able to get so many people from distant places to come to a five- or six-day party in Atlanta every year. The answer lies in the annual invitation. Each year had to top the year before.

My favorite invitation had to be the one from 1986. In July of that year, I created a fictitious organization called the Lombardo Foundation, named after famed bandleader Guy Lombardo, and I declared Wm. J. Boolie III as its president. Then I rented a PO Box. Finally, I sent a letter to nine famous people, which said:

As the current president of the Lombardo Foundation, it is my pleasure to inform you about our annual meeting, which will be held in Atlanta this year. Since its founding two years ago, the Foundation has built a solid record of public service. Our goals continue to embrace traditional values and spiritual renewal.

We will be holding our annual meeting in December and have selected Atlanta as the site. There will be representatives from at least ten states and two foreign countries at the meeting. We are excited about this opportunity to review the progress made during 1986 and discuss our plans for 1987.

I would very much appreciate a letter of welcome from your office to the delegates. Given the opportunity to showcase the city of Atlanta and the state of Georgia, it strikes me that such a letter would be quite appropriate.

Thank you in advance for your prompt consideration.

Sincerely,

Wm. J. Boolie III

Personal letters were sent to President Ronald Reagan, Georgia Senators Sam Nunn and Matt Mattingly, Georgia Congressman Wyche Fowler, Georgia Governor Joe Frank Harris, Atlanta Mayor Andrew Young, Jerry Falwell, and Ted Turner.

Two responded that they needed more information about the Foundation before they could write an introductory letter. But my guy, Senator Sam Nunn, really came through.

United States Senate
WASHINGTON, D.C. 20510

July 31, 1986

Dear William:

I am delighted to welcome you and the
members of the Lombardo Foundation to Atlanta
for your Annual Meeting.

The members of the Lombardo Foundation
have built a solid record of public service
since its founding two years ago. I admire
and respect your goals to embrace traditional
values and spiritual renewal. Your review of
the past year's progress and your discussion
of your plans for 1987 should stimulate a
thoughtful focus on the future of the
Lombardo Foundation.

Best wishes for a successful meeting and
an enjoyable stay in Atlanta.

Sincerely,

Sam Nunn

Mr. William J. Boolie, III
President
The Lombardo Foundation
P.O. Box 467582
Atlanta, Georgia 30346

Gone Fishin'

In 1991, I had relocated from Booz Allen's Atlanta office to their New York office and was leading the global service operations practice. This was one of the fastest growing practice areas in the firm, and I was woefully short of partners to focus on it. Our new partners came up through the ranks and were elected from the existing senior staff 95 percent of the time. But I didn't have enough coming through the pipeline to take advantage of the opportunities that we had, so I decided to bring in two partners from the outside.

These are tough positions to fill. An outside partner hire has to be a solid, experienced, and capable professional to earn the trust and confidence of the staff and to earn the respect of the existing partner corps. So I worked hard to find two partners who could and would be successful. I'm proud to say that I succeeded. John Devereaux joined from Deloitte & Touche and Roy King joined from KPMG Peat Marwick. Both got immediate traction and became fully integrated into the practice and into the culture of the firm. Even better, during the interview process, I learned that Roy was an avid fisherman.

I am not a great fisherman, but I can hold my own. My first memory of lake fishing was with my dad and my grandfather in maybe 1961 in a rowboat on Lake Erie. It was the height of the perch season. As I remember, we caught six hundred fish in maybe six hours. We were anchored right on top of a huge school and were catching them as fast as we could bait our hook and get our line back in the water.

When I was older, my folks bought a cottage by a small lake in eastern Ohio. I would sit on their dock and fish by the hour when I visited. Sometimes I just wanted the serenity of the beautiful weather and the relaxation of having a line in the water, so I wouldn't even bother to bait the hook. Actually catching a fish would have interrupted the peacefulness.

Shortly after Roy joined the firm, he and I planned our first fly-in fishing trip to Quebec, Canada. This was to be the first of eight such trips between 1991 and 1999. On each trip, we would fly to Montreal, rent an SUV, drive for three hours due north to a little town named Sainte-Anne-du-Lac, and stay at a local motel. The next morning, we would hop on a chartered seaplane; fly for another hour due north, and land at one of several lakes, far into the Northwoods.

Seven times we went to Baie du Nord, which is a large body of water, 350 miles north of Montreal. There was not even a road within fifty miles in any direction. The bay is maybe twenty-five miles long and fifteen miles wide. It is well-stocked with walleye and northern pike.

At the south end of the bay there were eight cabins, although rarely were more than two of them occupied. These were not luxurious cabins. Each of them would sleep four to eight people. Each had a propane stove, a propane refrigerator/freezer, and a propane heater. Seven had hand pumps to provide water straight from the bay, and required the use of an outhouse. But the eighth cabin had indoor plumbing, including a toilet, a shower, running water, and a hot water heater. We took that cabin every chance we could.

The air charter and the cabins were owned and operated by an outfitter named Réal Melançon and his company, Air Melançon. Réal was a rugged outdoorsman. I remember that one of the first times we were flying in, Réal was our pilot. I asked him, "So what happens if one of us has a heart attack up here?"

"You die," he responded matter-of-factly.

"What?" I said.

"You die. There is no means of communication. It's too far to walk for help. You're toast. We try to fly over every couple of days to check on you. In your cabin, you'll find a big aluminum sheet with a red cross on it. Put that out on the dock, and if we see it, we will land. But I doubt that we would be there in time if you had a massive heart attack."

I later decided that if I had to die, this wouldn't be a bad place to have it happen.

In June of 1996, Mike Wheeler, a colleague from Cleveland, joined Roy and me for four days of fishing. It was a great trip and we all fared well. The most exciting catch was made by Mike—or I should say it started with Mike. I'll explain: Walleye tend to congregate where the water temperature is about 58°. On this trip, that was at a water depth of about eighteen feet. Northern pike, on the other hand, are ambush predators. They tend to hide in shallow water around reeds and weeds, and then, when they see dinner coming by, they use their remarkable acceleration to overtake and strike their prey. It's pretty dramatic.

We had been fishing all morning for walleye at the appropriate depth. At about noon, we decided to go in for lunch and began reeling in our lines. Mike's bait was coming up from eighteen feet, and when it got to about three feet—bam! A northern strike! The line flew out of his reel as the northern headed away from the boat and straight toward the bottom, trying to escape.

Now, we need a time-out to explain some things. First, a northern pike has a wicked set of very sharp teeth. Many fishermen get badly cut trying to get them off of their lines. Second, about the only way to catch a northern is to use a steel leader, wherein the first six inches of the line above the hook are made of steel so the fish can't simply bite through the line. Third, fishing line is rated by its tested weight capacity. Four-pound test should not break if the fish being caught is less than four pounds. Similarly, twenty-pound test should hold up to a twenty-pound fish. But you want to use the lightest test that you can to minimize the odds that the fish will sense the line.

Since we were fishing for walleye, which rarely get larger than four pounds, Mike was using four-pound test line. And since walleye don't have sharp teeth, he was not using a steel leader. Unfortunately, this northern pike turned out to be thirty-eight inches long, it weighed nineteen pounds, and it had a full set of razorlike choppers.

We quickly presumed that the fish must have been hooked on his lip, outside of his mouth; otherwise, he would have easily bit through the line. This turned out to be correct when we finally landed him. That meant Mike had to keep the line taut so the fish couldn't get its teeth on it. Then there was the issue of the four-pound test line. The only way to land this guy would be to let him completely tire himself out. If Mike tried too hard to reel him in, the line would simply snap.

It took forty-five minutes to successfully get this rascal into the boat. It was both physically and mentally demanding, so Mike, Roy, and I traded off. In a true team effort, we finally landed him. Avid fishermen are very envious right now: a twenty-pound northern pike on four-pound test and no steel leader. Match that.

Baie du Nord has some of the best walleye and northern pike fishing in the world. That's where Roy and I went on our first four and our last three trips. But in 1995, we decided to try a new place named Sand Lake. This is a very small lake that by reputation had lots of lake trout, as well as plenty of walleye and pike. At that time, there was only one cabin that didn't yet have indoor plumbing. This place required really roughing it.

We arrived at Sand Lake on May 23. According to Réal, our outfitter, the ice had come off of the lake only nine days earlier, on May 14. Now, soon after the ice comes off of a lake is when most fish spawn. And walleye are no exception. For walleye to spawn, the water temperature needs to be between 40° and 44°. That usually means one to two weeks after the ice melts. And, as we were about to learn, walleye aren't big feeders while the spawning process is going on.

We landed at Sand Lake at ten in the morning and had our lines in the water just after eleven. I caught a nice 4½-pound, twenty-four-inch lake trout at a little after noon. And that was the last fish, the last bite, the last nibble we had all day. This was the first time Roy had been skunked in Canada in forty-one years.

Wednesday wasn't much better. In ten hours of fishing, Roy and I caught exactly five fish: two small northern pike, which we released, and three keeper walleye. While it was pretty slim pickings, those three walleye were the biggest we had ever caught in Canada: 3½ pounds, 3¾ pounds, and 4½ pounds.

Thursday, we got shut out again: no bites, no fights, and no fish. Clearly, we had shown up smack dab in the middle of spawning season. And there was nothing we could do but wait it out. We tried to set a romantic mood by lighting candles and humming Montovani music. We drew provocative pictures of naked fish and held them over the side of the boat. We tried everything we could think of to get the fish in the mood and move them along. But nothing worked.

On Friday, we hit the lake early. The plane was coming to pick us up at noon, and we had to be back to our cabin by 11:00 to get ready. As luck would have it, spawning season apparently ended at exactly 10:45 a.m. We caught a 4½-pound walleye at 10:47 a.m. and a 3½-pound walleye at 10:51 a.m. Then it was back to civilization. Oh, for two more days.

The Bronx Bombers

Die with memories, not dreams.

Cheap Suitcase

My good friend Frank Varasano and I are lifelong New York Yankees fans. We both trace our fandom back to the 1950s. In 1991, when I moved to the New York area, he and I decided that we really needed good season tickets to our beloved Bronx Bombers. Through a long and circuitous route involving the Yankee ticket office, my insurance broker, and multiple off-season visits to see Hank Sain, the Yankees senior vice president of ticket sales, we were able to land four season tickets in Field Box 60, six rows up from third base.

For the next fifteen years, Frank and I went to many games—usually together. Most years, we would see at least forty games. In 1996, I saw seventy-eight games and Frank saw ninety-two. Those included spring training games, regular season games, and postseason games. We were occasionally joined by Larry Roth, a mutual friend of many years. Larry is the biggest baseball fan on the planet. He attends maybe two hundred games a year: college, minor league, and major league. And he watched most of the major league ball players develop before they got to the "bigs."

Almost every year, Larry—who at the time was a confirmed bachelor from Chicago—would spend Christmas with Frank and his wife, Celene. During one of his visits in the mid-90s, the three of us established a new holiday tradition. Christmas Eve morning is sort of a dead time in holiday celebrating. There is rarely anything going on. So Frank, Larry, and I began an annual pilgrimage to pay tribute to the Bronx Bombers.

First, we would meet at a Greenwich, Connecticut, diner for breakfast. I can still taste the pancakes and sausage, and I can still remember Larry filling us in on all the off-season gossip: rumored trades, possible managerial changes, up-and-coming players.

After breakfast, we would drive to the Gate of Heaven Cemetery in Hawthorne, New York. Gate of Heaven is the cemetery for St. Patrick's Cathedral in New York City and is the final resting place for many, many famous people.

We always visited the graves of Yankee greats Babe Ruth and Billy Martin. It was amazing to see the remembrances left on their graves by earlier visitors: flowers, letters, pictures, baseballs, bats. And remember, this was at the end of December. After these visits, we often made quick stops at the graves of actor Jimmy Cagney and mobster Dutch Schultz. I don't know why we did this. It just seemed like a good idea at the time.

Then we would continue our pilgrimage by going to the Cathedral of Baseball, the House That Ruth Built: Yankee Stadium. After bluffing our way past security, we would visit Field Box 60 and look out over the diamond, imagining that it was opening day. What a time of joyful anticipation.

Then we would visit Hank Sain. Remember him? He was the senior vice president of ticket sales for the Yankees and a good man to know. George Steinbrenner used to make the entire Yankee staff work on Christmas Eve, so we figured it would be a good thing to stop by the ticket office and wish them a Merry Christmas. You can never have too many friends in a ticket office.

In 1997, we followed the same ritual: breakfast, Babe, Billy, and the Bronx. When we got to the stadium, we needed to get past the security guard. I whispered to Frank and Larry to follow my lead and strode confidently up to the front desk.

I said to the guard, in a voice that sounded like I owned the place, "We have a meeting in two minutes with Hank Sain. Do you want to be the reason we're late?"

"Right through those doors, gentlemen, down the hallway on the right," said the guard.

"Thank you, sir," I replied, and off we went.

Our first stop was, of course, Field Box 60. But as we were looking out at the field, we noticed a group of workmen doing something in front of the stands between the dugouts. As we walked closer, it became apparent that they were pouring cement to create a new front row of seats.

"Holy Shit!" said Frank.

"Oh my God!" said Larry.

"Sain!" said I. "We gotta go see Hank Sain." And off we went.

We hustled to the ticket office to try to get our hands on four season tickets in the new front row. The following is what transpired next:

Clerk: "May I help you?"

Me: "Yes, please. We're here to see Hank Sain."

Clerk: "I'm sorry, but he is on the phone. Can someone else help you?"

Me: "No, thanks. We'll wait."

We had been standing in the lobby for maybe ten minutes when a nice-looking young man came out and introduced himself as Elmer, the assistant director of ticket sales.

Elmer: "Are you sure I can't help you? Mr. Sain is still on the phone."

Me: "No, that's all right. We'll wait."

Elmer: "He's on a call with George Steinbrenner. It could last for a couple of hours."

Me: "Well, Elmer, we saw them pouring concrete down on the field, and it looks like you are putting in a new front row of seats. Is that right?"

Elmer: "Yep. They're going to be called the Legend Seats, and they'll only be sixty-four of them. But I doubt that you'll be interested. They are going to be crazy expensive."

Me: "Well, Elmer, we are very interested."

Elmer: "How many seats might you be interested in?"

Me: "All of them."

Elmer: "All of them? I'll be right back!"

And he took off running for Sain's office. About three minutes later, Hank walked around the corner and saw us standing there.

"Oh hell, it's just you guys!" he said.

"Well, Merry Christmas to you, Hank," Frank said.

"Okay, let's take a walk," he replied.

During our walk to the new seats, Hank suggested that he owed us big time, saying, "I was on the phone with the boss. There is nothing worse than getting chewed out by George Steinbrenner on Christmas Eve."

"When my guy told me that someone was interested in all of the Legend Seats, I said to George, 'Do you want me to sit here listening to you scream at me, or do you want me to go sell some tickets?' He said, 'Go sell tickets!' and promptly hung up the phone."

We finally made it down to the freshly poured concrete, and Hank began to point out the locations of the new seats. They would be priced at $200 per game and would come with a membership to the private Yankee Club and a pass for the player's parking lot.

Then he began to show us available locations. As he did, my buddy, Frank, was sizing up the situation. He finally said, "We want these four right here." They were in the front row on an aisle directly behind the visitor's on deck circle. They were perfect.

Hank responded, "Too bad. Steinbrenner has blocked them for his own use."

Then Larry weighed in. "Perhaps Mr. Varasano wasn't clear. While the other options are wonderful seats, Frank said that we want these four seats right here."

"I'll talk to George. He always folds when money is on the line. I'll call you," Sain offered. And with that, he walked away.

Two days after Christmas, I was having some tasty eggnog when the phone rang. The conversation was short and completely one-sided: "Krauss, Sain. Steinbrenner folded like a cheap suitcase. The seats are yours. Send me a check." Click.

The Duck

In "Cheap Suitcase," I told the story of how my buddy Frank Varasano and I came to acquire four season tickets in the Legend Seats at Yankee Stadium beginning in the 1998 season. These seats were just possibly the best four seats in the stadium. They were in the first row. They had extra legroom. They were big and cushioned. They abutted an aisle. We kept those seats for eleven years until they built and opened the new Yankee Stadium in 2009.

Most of the season ticket holders on the visitor's side of the Legend Seats were a close-knit group. Almost all the seats were owned by individuals, not corporations. Most owners came to at least half or more of the games. Some, like us, showed up 80 percent of the time. Hence, everyone knew everyone pretty well. There was a lot of camaraderie among this group of folks.

The four seats next to us were occupied by Big Jim Scibelli, a great guy who lived on Long Island. Jimmy was larger than life, in more ways than one. He was a very large man. He was also extroverted, funny, and a real jokester. He was always teasing and laughing and having fun. Jimmy enjoyed life. He was a successful investor and owner of a large, successful black car service in the New York Metro area. But he always left work behind when he came to a ball game. More on Jimmy later.

The four seats to our right were owned by the managing partner of a law firm in Bridgeport, Connecticut. He had a long distance to travel to the stadium, so he gave away a lot of his tickets. But we saw him at most weekend games and at almost every postseason game.

To his right, Lorne Michaels, the producer of *Saturday Night Live* had four seats. He was a huge fan, and we saw him at almost every game. He also brought some pretty interesting guests.

It was the second game of the World Series in 2000: the Yankees against the Mets. Lorne Michaels had brought royalty to the game: Sir Paul McCartney. Now I am not one who often gets starstruck—but I was by Sir Paul. He's one of the Beatles, for crying out loud. When *Meet the Beatles* was released in January of 1964, I was a freshman in high school. I was more than a big fan; I was a participant in the pop music revolution, which was led by Paul McCartney and the Beatles.

I've frequently been around famous people and find them to be just like you and me: some are nice, some are funny, some are jerks. But most are good people, and they have learned to put up with the inconvenience of being famous.

Sir Paul is such a person. He was seated only five seats away from us, and when we waved and said hello before the game started, he waved back and said, "Hey, guys." During the game, he would join in our cheers and our jeers. He acted just like one of the guys: an old pal takin' in the ball game.

Now during the 2000 postseason, Big Jim Scibelli brought his lucky yellow duck to each game. Whenever the Yankees really needed a hit or a run or an out, Jimmy would put the duck on the wall in front of us and we would all pass our hands over it and say our chants to release its magic spirits. The duck was pretty effective; during the 2000 postseason, the Yanks were 5–2 at home.

To be safe, Big Jim used the duck at the beginning of game two. But Dave Justice and Bernie Williams scored in the first inning, and the duck went back in Jim's pocket.

Meanwhile, Roger Clemens was pitching lights out. For the game, Roger went eight innings and gave up two hits, no walks, and no runs. He struck out nine. Then it got interesting. With the

Yankees leading by six going into the ninth inning and with Roger scheduled to pitch game six, if it came to that, manager Joe Torre decided to give him a rest. He brought in Jeff Nelson to close out the game. Jeff promptly gave up three hits and two runs without registering an out. Out came the duck.

With one man on base and a four-run lead, Torre went to the bullpen for The Man: Mariano Rivera, the best relief pitcher to ever play the game. Mo came into the stadium, as he always did, to the sound of Metallica's "Enter Sandman." After giving up a ground ball single to Benny Agbayani, the Mets had two men on base. The duck was on center stage. Mo got Lenny Harris to hit into a fielder's choice. Now he had two outs and a four-run lead. This should have been a piece of cake for the great Mariano. But the duck stayed right where he was.

Jay Payton walked to the plate. Mo had a 1–1 count and challenged Payton with a 94 mph fastball. Jay waited on it and waited on it and waited on it and *pow*... a line drive home run into the right field corner. That made the score Yankees 6 – Mets 5. We were going crazy, but the duck never looked more confident. We pointed toward the pitcher's mound and whispered "Strike out. Strike out. Strike out." Sure enough, Mariano got Kurt Abbott to strike out looking. The Yankees win!

As we were walking to our cars after the game, Frank said to me, "So who was the MVP of the game?"

"I vote for Mariano. He got the last clutch out," I replied.

"No," said Frank. "It's gotta be Clemens, who gave up two hits and no runs over eight innings and won the game."

Unbeknownst to us, Sir Paul was walking behind us. "You're both wrong," McCartney countered in his distinctive British accent. "It was the fucking duck!"

Mister Mayor

Partly because we were huge Yankee fans and partly because our seats were so good, my pal Frank and I went to lots of ball games: fifty or sixty a year was common. And because we were there so much, we knew lots and lots of people. Other season ticket holders, Yankee executives, the beer man, security guards, and even some of the grounds crew knew us by name.

As an example of this, Frank—who lived in Glen Cove, Long Island—forgot his parking pass, his Yankee Club pass, and his ticket one day, and he was almost to the stadium when he realized it. He decided to press on.

One of the great benefits of having Legend Seats tickets was that they came with a parking pass for the player's lot, directly across the street from the stadium entrance. Frank pulled into the lot and stopped at the gate.

"Louie, I had a brain freeze this morning," he said to the attendant. "I forgot my pass."

"No problem, Frank," Louie answered. "Park wherever you want."

Then Frank crossed the street and approached the ticket turnstile.

"Rocco," he said to the head ticket taker, "I left today's ticket at home. It's sitting on my dresser."

"Not a problem, Frank. I know who you are. Come on in," Rocco replied.

Then Frank went upstairs to the Yankee Club, a private bar and restaurant inside Yankee Stadium and our usual pregame haunt. And once again, he was admitted without his pass, a rare event when security Nazi Mary Ellen was working the door.

Finally, just before the game started, he went to our seats. Because these were prime seats and lots of fans tried to sneak into the section, the area was chained off and a security guard checked everyone's ticket when they came through.

Once again, Frank said, "Sorry, Roberto, no ticket today. I forgot and left it at home."

Once again, the guard said, "No problem, Frank. Come right in."

Now this whole deal would have been a nice surprise in Milwaukee or Seattle or San Diego. But in New York City, it was unprecedented. To get past one ticket taker and three pass checkers was nothing short of amazing. As regulars, we were always acknowledged and afforded great consideration.

One of the people who looked after us in the front row was a man named Willie, who was a member of the grounds crew. He would keep things picked up and take care of any issues that the Legends Seats fans might have during the game.

One time before the start of a Thursday night game, I was in my seat talking with Frank about the evening's pitching matchup, when Willie yelled to me, "Hey, Kurt; come over here for a minute."

I got up and walked over to where Willie was standing and immediately recognized the huge man that was standing next to him. It was seven-time, All-Pro, and eventual Pro Football Hall of Famer Warren Sapp.

"Kurt," Willie said, "I'd like you to meet Warren Sapp. Warren, this is Kurt Krauss. Kurt is the mayor of the front row here at Yankee Stadium."

"I'm honored to meet you, Kurt," Warren said. "Just what does being mayor of the front row entail?"

"Well, Warren," I answered, "first, I have to make sure that everyone seated in the front row is a real baseball fan. They have to understand and appreciate the game. Second, I have to ensure that everyone down here is a true Yankee fan. We don't want to be seen with Red Sox fans or Oriole fans. They are not nice people, and they smell funny. Finally, it falls to me to get the front row screamin' and hollerin' when the Yankees need a little support. But given how many die-hard fans sit down here, that's a pretty easy job."

"Wow!" said Warren. "I had no idea."

Willie was standing a little behind Warren, and it was all he could do not to break out laughing.

"By the way, Warren," I said, "you do know baseball and you are a Yankee fan, right?"

"I do and I am, sir. You have nothing to worry about from me."

"That's what I like to hear. Warren, you enjoy the game." And I walked back to my seat.

These kinds of things were regular occurrences for Frank and me. The entertainment value was very high in the Legends Seats. To end my Warren Sapp story, the Yankees were up by maybe seven runs in the eighth inning, and I decided to get a jump on the postgame traffic. As I stood and turned to walk up the steps and leave, I heard a shout from my left.

Warren stood and yelled, "Good-bye, Mister Mayor. Have a nice evening."

"You too, Warren; see you next time," I yelled back.

Many treasured memories of the stadium involve Lorne Michaels and the friends he would bring to the games. As you probably know, Lorne was, and still is, the executive producer of *Saturday Night Live.* He is also an avid Yankee fan.

Lorne's seats were only five away from ours, and he would often show up with somebody famous. I got a chance to meet many interesting people including Paul McCartney, Jack Nicholson, Jimmy Fallon, P. Diddy, Jennifer Lopez, Lorraine Bracco, Penny Marshall, Cameron Diaz, and Paul Simon.

The first time I met Jack Nicholson turned out to be a real hoot. I was at a World Series game in 1998 when I noticed him standing next to Lorne with his back to me maybe ten minutes before the game was due to start. I walked up and tapped him on the shoulder.

He spun around, clearly afraid that he was going to be hassled. I said, "Relax, Jack. I just wanted to introduce myself and ask you a couple of questions on behalf of the New York Yankees. My name is Kurt Krauss, and I just want to be sure that you are a baseball fan, and more importantly, that you are a Yankee fan."

"What the hell are you talking about?" Jack screamed. "I grew up in New Jersey, and I've been a Yankees fan since 1949. You see this hat?" he asked, removing his ball cap. "I've had it since the mid-1950s. Don't question my loyalty."

"Geez, Jack," I answered weakly, "I didn't mean to piss you off. I've been a Yankees fan since 1959, so I understand something about loyalty. I just get tired of seeing so many celebrity interlopers who wouldn't know a baseball from a Buick showing up for World Series games and pretending to be an 'insider.' So I appointed myself mayor, and I try to shame them away from the front-row seats. Do you know what I'm getting at?"

"I do," he said. "I see it all of the time at Laker's games. I appreciate what you are trying to do. Enjoy the game." And he turned and went back to his seat.

The Yankees won the game. The next morning, there was a picture from the game on the front page of the sport's section of the *New York Times*. It must have been taken from the center field bleachers with a powerful zoom-lens camera, because it showed the Yankees catcher running back to the screen trying to catch a foul ball that had been popped up behind home plate. You could clearly see the catcher, and the ball was about one foot above his glove, ready to be caught.

You could also see the fans in the seats behind the screen who were all completely concentrating on the play unfolding in front of them. On the left edge of the shot, there was Jack Nicholson with his eyes riveted on the ball. Interestingly, all the other fans sitting around him were still staring up in the air, where the ball had been two seconds earlier. It looked like they were stargazing. I cut out the picture and tucked it in my wallet.

That night, I went to the next play-off game at the stadium, and who should be back but Jack. Before the game started, I walked over and kneeled down in front of him.

"Hey, Jack," I said.

"Hey, buddy," he replied. From that point forward, every time I saw Jack, he referred to me as "buddy."

"Jack, do you remember last night when I pissed you off by questioning whether or not you were a real baseball fan?" I asked.

"I do," he replied.

"Well, did you read the *New York Times* today? There was a picture from last night's game that bears directly on the matter."

"No, I didn't see a paper today. What did the picture show?"

"It shows that you were the only die-hard fan sitting in your section," I offered, pulling the picture out of my wallet and unfolding it. "Do you remember this play from last night's game?" I asked.

"I sure do."

"Well, there you are. And what are you looking directly at?" I queried.

"I'm looking right at the ball as the catcher gets ready to catch it."

"Right," I said. "And where are all of the rest of the fans looking?"

"They're looking up in the sky."

"That's right, Jack. You are looking at the ball, while everyone else is stargazing. I'd say that you are the only proven baseball fan in the group."

Jack beamed and smiled as only Jack Nicholson can do as I continued. "And the best part, Jack, is that we now have photographic evidence of your behavior."

He continued to beam when Lorne, who was sitting next to him, said, "I wasn't gazing up in the air, Jack. I was also watching the ball."

Most of Lorne's body had been cropped out of the photo, and you could not see his face. "Unfortunately, Lorne," Jack responded, "we have absolutely no photographic evidence. And we can't just take your word for it."

"Thanks, buddy," Jack said to me. It seems that I was back in his good graces.

Another time, Jack wore a pair of shoes that could only be described as strange. They were brown with irregular beige splotches all over them. Between innings, I looked down the row and said, "Hey, Jack. What's up with the shoes?"

"Do you like 'em?" he responded. "I made them myself."

They broke the mold when they made Jack Nicholson.

I was involved in other Mister Mayor moments over the years. But the one that stands out was an encounter with Reverend Jesse Jackson.

By now, you know that the Legend Seats were special. There was even a concrete section behind the seats that was maybe three feet wide to keep the fans in the old front row from breathing down our necks. In play-off games, the Yankees put folding chairs in that section and sold the tickets for $1000 each.

It was yet another World Series game, and we all had assembled in our seats maybe twenty minutes before the game was to start. Just then, I noticed Reverend Jackson coming down the stairs toward our seats. He made it all the way to the folding chair catty-cornered behind us and started to settle in. Time for some fun, I thought.

I walked over to him and said, "Reverend Jackson, welcome to Yankee Stadium. I'm Kurt Krauss, and I am the duly appointed mayor of the front row. I just need to ask you a couple of questions."

Ten or so of my friends who were seated near us knew what was coming and began to move closer to us, effectively hemming Jesse in.

"So, Jesse," I asked, "I need to know if you are a real baseball fan."

"Oh yes," Jesse said. "Baseball is my favorite sport by far."

"That's great," I offered. "And I trust that you are a Yankee fan."

"I sure am," he said. "I have been a Yankee fan for my whole life."

"Okay, we're almost done," I said. "This isn't the first game that you've attended a game in person this year, is it?"

"Not a chance," he replied. "I've probably been to at least ten games this year."

"You mean that you've been to Yankee Stadium ten times this year? That's terrific," I responded.

"Oh no," he said. "I was at Comiskey Park in Chicago ten times," he admitted. "This is my first time at Yankee Stadium this year."

"Oh, Reverend Jackson," I explained. "If this is your first visit to the stadium this year, then you are not allowed to sit in these seats." I turned and pointed into the upper deck nosebleed seats. "I'm afraid you're going to have to sit up there. They have a section reserved for people like you who failed to support the team during the regular season. And if you just show them your ticket for this seat, they will find you alternate seating."

"I'm not sitting up there! I have a ticket for this seat right here," Jessie yelled, pointing at his folding chair.

"You really don't have a choice, Reverend Jackson," I said in a calm voice. "I'm very sorry, but those are the rules. In order to sit in the front-row seats, you have to be a true Yankee fan and you have to have been to at least three regular season games this year. Otherwise, you're nothing more than a famous person who shows up at big events just to be seen. We need real fans in these seats."

"I'm not going to move," he continued to insist. "I'm sitting right here.

"Please don't make me call security, Reverend Jackson," I countered.

At just that moment, I looked over Jessie's shoulder, and who should I see walking up to us but Chuck Schumer, the US senator from New York?

"Hi, Jesse, it's good to see you," he said. "I've got four seats on the other side foul screen, and I'm by myself. Do you want to sit with me?"

"I sure do, Chuck. Thanks," he said in a relieved tone of voice.

The two of them walked over to the first base side of the field and sat in Chuck Schumer's front-row seats. The two other seats went empty for the whole game. I've often thought what a nerdy guy Chuck Schumer must have been to have had four front-row seats to a World Series game in Yankee Stadium and not be able to get anyone to go with him. Poor schmuck!

Mister Daddy

The thrills were frequent in the Legend Seats at Yankee Stadium. It was October 1999, and we were playing the Atlanta Braves in the World Series. I was there with my partners, Frank Varasano and Joe Fisher. Frank and I went back thirty years and had grown up together at Booz Allen Hamilton. I got to know Joe when I was the CFO of Burson-Marsteller, the global PR agency, and he was the CEO of the US business. We had known one another for only three years, but we had grown to be very good friends.

The three of us were joined by Ralph Welch—known to us as the Welcher—another former Booz Allen partner and, at that time, the COO of multibillion-dollar technology company. Ralph, Frank, and I were close friends for years, although some unfortunate behavior by Ralph in 2010 severed our friendship with him. Suffice it to say that he is no longer on either of our Christmas card lists.

But in 1999, all was good. As we took our seats and got ready for the player introductions that are made before the first World Series game in each team's home stadium, we heard a bit of commotion behind us. Rap star Sean Combs, known to the world as Puff Daddy, and actress Jennifer Lopez were sitting down in the row behind us in seats that were catty-corner across the aisle from us. I knew at once that we would have some fun on this night.

Nothing significant happened for the first couple of innings. But between the second and third inning, Ralph turned around and spoke to the rap star.

"What do I call you?" Ralph asked.

"What do you mean?" was the response.

"Well, do I call you Sean, or Mister Combs, or Puff, or Puff Daddy, or Mister Daddy?" Ralph explained.

"My friends call me Puffy," Mister Daddy answered. [Note: I should point out that I fell in love with the name "Mister Daddy," and I have used it ever since.]

"Then can I call you Puffy?" Ralph continued.

"I would be honored," Mister Daddy replied.

"Okay, Puffy, will you say hello to my daughter?"

"Sure," Mister Daddy answered. "Where is she?"

"She's in Texas," Ralph said as he pulled out his cell phone and dialed her number.

When she answered, Ralph simply said, "Honey, someone here at the game wants to say hello," and he handed Mister Daddy his phone.

Mister Daddy was cool. He talked to Ralph's daughter for probably five minutes. When he handed the phone back, Ralph said, "Thanks, man, I really appreciate it."

"No problem," Mister Daddy said. "I was happy to do it."

In about the fourth inning, Ralph left to use the restroom. I then had a short, but very insightful conversation with Mister Daddy.

After Ralph left, I turned to Mister Daddy and said, "Do you know whose daughter you just spoke with?"

"Sure," he replied. "He's Ralph Welch, chief operating officer of Data Base Corporation."

"How in the hell do you know that, Puffy?" I asked.

"I manage my investments closely, man," Mister Daddy replied.

Blow me over with a feather. This changed my entire perception of him. As I have followed the rap star over the years, I have always found him to be a shrewd and savvy businessman.

At the end of the fifth inning, my buddies and I decided to visit the Yankee Club and say hello to a bunch of friends. The Yankee Club was a private hideaway located in the middle of Yankee

Stadium. It had a very good restaurant and an even better bar. Suffice it to say that we were regulars.

The maître d' was named George Tracy, or just Tracy to his friends. We were all about the same age, and we got along famously from the first time we met. We had become, and remain to this day, very good friends. We talked to Tracy at length before every game, and we made it a point to visit him at least once during each game.

The Yanks were losing 5–2 when we got to the club, so we spent some time with Tracy and the bartender, Danny Sullivan, convincing each other that we had the Braves right where we wanted them and that there was no way Atlanta's bullpen would hold the Bombers to only five runs. That turned out to be true. Chuck Knoblauch blasted a two run homer in the eighth inning to tie the game, and Chad Curtis hit his second home run of the night in the bottom of the eleventh to win the game 6–5.

After our powwow, I walked through the club saying hello to various friends and acquaintances. As I made my way back to the bar area, I noticed Danny Sullivan trying to get my attention. When I got closer, he began to point toward the far end of the bar. By then I could see that Yankee Hall of Famer, Whitey Ford, was sitting at the end of the bar with his son Eddie, watching the game on TV. Danny and I approached them from different sides of the bar. When we got close, Danny introduced us.

"Whitey, Eddie, this is a longtime Yankee fan Kurt Krauss. Kurt, this is Whitey Ford and his son Eddie."

I have been a huge New York Yankee fan since 1960, when I first saw them play in Cleveland. Yogi Berra, Mickey Mantle, and Whitey Ford were my three idols. And now I was actually meeting Whitey in person.

"Whitey, you pitched in the first game I ever saw back in 1960, almost fifty years ago," I opened with.

"Was it here at the stadium?" he asked.

"No, it was in Cleveland at the old Municipal Stadium," I answered.

"Did I win?" he continued.

"No, Eddie Lopat got the win. But you pitched two innings and got the save. It was one of only eleven in your career. No hits, no runs, no walks, three strikeouts," I said. "Pretty impressive."

"Well, thank God for that," Whitey replied.

We made some small talk about baseball and the Yankees and his old teammates. And then I pointed up to the TV. Jason Grimsley was pitching for the Yankees in the sixth inning.

"So what do you think of Grimsley?" I asked.

"He'll never amout to squat."

"Why not?"

"Because he doesn't cheat."

Whitey apparently believed in stretching the rule book in order to get an advantage over the batter. He once told ESPN that he threw a "gunk" ball that combined a mixture of baby oil, turpentine, and resin, which he kept in a roll-on dispenser.

Meeting my childhood idol was a real treat, one that I will never forget.

It had been about thirty minutes since we had left our seats, and it was time to get back. As we walked down the stairs leading to the front row, I noticed that two of our seats were occupied. Damn, I thought, until I realized that it was Mister Daddy and JLo. I came up behind them and tapped them on the shoulder.

"Excuse me," I said.

"Oh, sorry. We'll move right now," JLo said, and she and Mister Daddy went back to their original seats.

We went back to watching the ball game and urging the Yankees toward a comeback. Between innings, I motioned for Mister Daddy to come over to me, which he did.

"Puffy, you really covet these front-row seats, don't you? I could see it in your eyes when we came back last inning," I asked.

"You're right, I do covet them," he replied. "There is just something about being in the front row at Yankee Stadium for a World Series game."

"Well I have a deal for you, and if you take it, you can sit with us during the World Series next year," I offered.

"What's the deal?" Mister Daddy said hopefully.

"Frank, Joe, and I own these seats, and we all believe strongly that the people who deserve to sit here are the true fans who love the Yankees and who come to at least a few regular season games during the year," I explained.

"Therefore," I continued, "we will give you one ticket to each World Series home game next year if, and only if, you join us for three regular season games. Two must be in April, and one can be in July or August."

"Do they have to be April?" he asked.

"Absolutely!" I said. "That's when the die-hard fans show up. You've got to be a real fan to sit here and watch a game in 35° weather." The ninth inning was getting ready to start, so I said, "What's it going to be? Are you in?"

"I'm in," Mister Daddy said. "Give me your phone number, and I'll call you in March."

I gave him my number and wondered if he would ever call. The next evening at a family dinner, I told Bonita and the children that Puff Daddy and I were going to go to a couple of ball games next year and that he was going to call me to set it up.

"If you answer a call from someone claming to be Puff Daddy, don't hang up. It is not a prank call," I said.

Unfortunately, I never heard back from him about those April games.

91

Booz Brothers

Check yourself into the Hokey Pokey Clinic and turn yourself around.

After-Party

$\mathbf{M}$y defining career was as a partner at the management consulting firm of Booz Allen Hamilton. In the seventies and eighties, consulting was the place to be. Investment banking hadn't yet reached the cachet it would soon attain. Law was, well, the law. At that time, management consulting was the top of the heap: the best and the brightest and all that nonsense.

It was very difficult to get a job offer from Booz Allen, as it was from the other blue-chip management consulting firms like McKinsey and the Boston Consulting Group. The odds were something like this: for every thirty candidates who were interviewed, only one got a job offer. And for every twenty folks who were hired, only one was eventually elected to the partnership. Tough odds. With a lot of hard work and a little luck, I was fortunate enough to make it over both of those hurdles.

The work was demanding at Booz Allen. Twelve-hour days were the norm. Travel was onerous: usually four to five days a week. But the work was challenging and stimulating and rewarding. It was a real high that made all the personal and physical demands pale by comparison.

We also had some fun along the way. The partners and staff in each office were usually a tight-knit group—professionally, personally, and socially. One of the annual social highlights was the Black-Tie Dinner Dance, which every office typically held in the spring. These were first-class affairs that never disappointed. And of course, some memories were made and some legends were born.

In the late 1970s, I was part of the Cleveland office. Our annual dinner dance was hosted by our managing partner, Jack McGrath, and his wife, Mary Ann, at the Canterbury Country Club in Shaker Heights. These were classy affairs, and Jack and Mary Ann were gracious hosts. But the thing that I remember most clearly about these parties is the band. Every year we had a dance band that was a real throwback to the 1950s. They reminded me of the Lawrence Welk Orchestra. The musicians had those cardboard bandstands with musical notes on the front. The band was good, but they were definitely a relic.

Jack took a lot of guff about the band. We told him that it was time to move the party into the 1970s. We said that we were certain that the band leader had to be his brother-in-law. We told him that we'd find the band next year. We told him that we'd pay for the band next year. It was all to no avail. He stood by his convictions. I came to believe that Jack had a mental image of what a first-class party looked and sounded like, and that his image was timeless. His band played on.

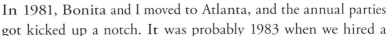

In 1981, Bonita and I moved to Atlanta, and the annual parties got kicked up a notch. It was probably 1983 when we hired a great guy named Bob Morin, from the University of Virginia. As I recall, Bob started on May 1, two weeks before that year's formal dinner dance. So of course, he came to the party.

I was on my way back from the restroom when I noticed that Bob was dancing with my wife. As I walked past them, Bob leaned over and whispered in my ear, "I've got my eye on your office too!"

Imagine that, out of a two-week rookie. While I cracked up on the spot, I was forced to put Bob on double secret probation for his unseemly behavior. Of course, that didn't last too long. Bob and I went on to become good friends, and we remain so today, thirty-three years later.

In the late 1980s, I took over as the managing partner of the Atlanta office. When party time rolled around, I decided that it was time for something new. I think it was in 1989 that our band was the Coasters. Remember them? They sang "Yakety Yak" and "Charlie Brown" back in the late 1950s.

Then, in 1990, I brought in the Drifters. Remember "Save the Last Dance for Me" and "Up on the Roof" from the early 1960s? One of their most famous songs is "Under the Boardwalk." Midway through the evening, when everyone was pretty well-lubed, four of us decided that we wanted to sing with the band. Bob Morin, Matt McKenna, Gary Shows, and I made do-rags out of our linen table napkins and went to the stage.

It was five black guys in brightly colored suits interspersed with four white guys in tuxedos and do-rags. But we did ourselves proud. "Under the Boardwalk" never sounded so good. What a memory.

The best party had to have been in 1985. Actually, the party was pretty tame. But the after-party was unbelievable. The formal party broke up around eleven. But for three of my partners and me, the night was still young. Gordy and Judy Ramseier, Walter and Becky Jewett, John and Laila Smith, and Bonita and I jumped into the limo we had reserved for the night and told the driver to take us straight to the Limelight——a popular club that opened in 1980 at the height of the disco craze. Here's a description of the place from Wikipedia:

> The Limelight in Atlanta was a high profile Euro-style night club that hosted many notables and

celebrities over the years. A single photo taken in June 1981 skyrocketed the focus on the club, when a celebrity photographer captured an image of Anita Bryant dancing the night away with evangelist Russ McGraw. Several hundred newspapers and magazines ran the photo with the headline "Anita Upset over Disco Photo."

When we arrived, the first thing we saw was a line of about two hundred people waiting to get into the club. The line stretched down the block and around the corner.

"Just pull up to the front door," I told the driver. "You guys wait here," I told my friends.

I got out of the limo and approached the bouncers behind the red velvet ropes. "Do you know who's in the limo?" I asked.

"No idea," said bouncer #1.

"Well, guys, we're the Moody Blues," I said.

"Come right this way," said bouncer #1.

"Go get the manager," shouted bouncer #2.

I stuck my head back in the car: "Showtime, folks. We are now officially the Moody Blues for the evening."

"Not a problem," the group responded.

I had chosen the Moody Blues specifically because I figured they were a band whose name everyone knew but whom no one recognized. Can you picture the Moody Blues right now? I didn't think so.

We were led in the door and greeted by the manager. "Welcome to the Limelight," he said. It was pretty clear that he had no idea what the real Moody Blues looked like, so in we went. We were offered a table in the front of the club and were served champagne on the house.

About a half hour after we arrived, the disc jockey stopped the music to make an announcement. "Ladies and gentlemen, joining us tonight are the Moody Blues. Let's give them a nice welcome."

With that the crowd began to clap and cheer. And we stood and waved to acknowledge them. What a moment. It was clear that not many people in that crowd knew what the Moody Blues looked like either. So we just went with the flow. We drank. We danced. We let the good times roll!

After about ninety minutes, we decided not to push our luck any further. We signed a few autographs and made our way to the exit, thanking the manager and the bouncers on our way out. Our limo was parked right where we had left it; so we piled in and headed for home.

It was truly a night to remember. Imagine—four management consulting partners became rock stars for a couple of hours. What a head spinner.

Cohiba!

I t was tough to get hired by a blue-chip management consulting firm during the late 1970s and 1980s. It was tougher yet to get promoted through the ranks and eventually be elected to the partnership. Most partners began life at Booz Allen Hamilton as entry-level associates. Typically, a new hire would have just been awarded a master's degree from one of the top business schools in the country. And he or she would have had at least three years of substantive work experience before going back to graduate school.

In order to have received a job offer from Booz Allen, the candidate would have been interviewed by at least ten or twelve different people, each having veto power over a potential job offer. It's no wonder that we considered maybe thirty candidates for every one that we hired.

It was equally tough to advance once you were hired. The standard progression was to be promoted from associate to senior associate to principal to partner. One generally spent two to three years in each of these positions. I estimate that only 40 percent of the associates, 25 percent of the senior associates, and 50 percent of the principals were promoted to the next level. That meant that walking in the door on your first day, you had about a 5 percent chance of going all the way.

People didn't make it for lots of reasons: Some received outside job offers that they couldn't pass up. Some found the travel and the lifestyle to be more of an issue than they originally thought it would be. Many were counseled to leave once it became clear that they were not going to make it to the next level. This "Up-or-Out" policy was necessary to keep the partner pipeline from becoming clogged and closing out high-potential players.

One way to improve the odds of successfully moving through the chairs was to have been a summer intern. Each year we would interview first-year MBA students from the top business schools in the country, and we would offer the best of the best a summer intern position with the firm. These positions were billed as a way for the candidate to learn about the consulting business and for the firm to learn about the candidate. If both sides were happy, a full-time job offer would be forthcoming at the end of the summer, and the intern would return to the firm when they graduated the following spring.

The reality was that these interns truly were the best at their respective schools. And they already knew that they wanted to play in the management consulting sandbox. About 95 percent of all summer interns received and accepted full-time offers.

My most memorable summer intern experience involved a guy that we hired out of Harvard Business School in 1987. His name was Rob Reese (pronounced Rees). His name was actually Robert Wentworth Reese III, but he preferred Rob.

Rob was a natural for the management consulting business in all dimensions but one. I used him on two of my client assignments over the summer, and he really stood out. He was smart. He was analytical. He was a good problem-solver. He was a good writer and a good communicator.

If he could have just overcome one nagging problem, Rob would have had a bright future at Booz Allen Hamilton. But his one nagging problem was that he was a total jerk. He was arrogant. He was full of himself. He had no ability to defer to the age or experience of others on any matter, be it social, professional, or personal.

One time I was in a meeting with my client service team, of which Rob was a part, and several senior client executives. I had explained to the CEO that his sales were far short of what they should have been, and I was in the process of articulating why this was so.

Then Rob interrupted me, saying, "Part of the problem is that the sales staff lacks any economic motivation to sell once they hit their monthly revenue targets."

No one else on the team had felt a need to take over my conversation. I seemed to be handling things pretty well. Including me, my team had over twenty years of consulting experience. Rob had twenty days.

The hell of it was that his comment was right. But he was way over the line in offering it up. He was a summer intern. Shut the hell up and learn from others.

Another time, two senior client executives had joined my team and me for dinner. After dinner, we retired to the cocktail lounge, where we proceeded to order a round of after-dinner drinks. When the drinks arrived, Rob opened up a $20 Cohiba cigar, lit it, sat back in his chair, propped his feet up on a nearby chair, and announced to the group, "This is the way God meant for people to live."

Now, both of the clients were in their fifties. I was in my forties. My team members were in their thirties. And here was Mr. Rob Reese, sharing his philosophy of life, at the ripe old age of twenty-four. It wasn't that he was wrong. It's that he one-upped the table with his Cohiba cigar, and then he acted like he was the most seasoned guy in the room with his profound declaration.

Over the summer, my colleagues and I tried to work with Rob to get his behavior at least into the tolerable zone. But it was all to no avail. He continued to act like an arrogant bozo. He was cocky and presumptuous and pretentious.

ASSHOLE IS NOT JUST A WORD ...
... IT'S A LIFESTYLE!

To be fair, when he made an observation, he was usually right. He was smart, and he was insightful. He brought a lot of value to the team and, by extension, to the client.

It was approaching time to decide whether or not to give him a permanent offer to join the firm as an associate the following spring when he graduated from Harvard. When I finally had to call the question, I summoned him to my office. I had an idea about how to deal with Rob's arrogance issue while still recognizing his talents and capabilities.

"So how was your summer experience, Rob?" I asked.

"It was great," he said. "I felt like I was able to contribute a lot on the two assignments I worked on. I really liked the intellectual challenge of the work."

"Do you think that you are a good fit for the firm, Rob?" I asked.

"Oh yes," he responded. "I got along great with all of the folks that I had the chance to work with. And I'm pretty sure that they thought that I was a good guy."

"Well, Rob," I said, "I agree that you would make a strong addition to our team, and I'd like to see you join us after you graduate. There is just one caveat to your job offer. You can't start until September."

"But I graduate in May. What am I supposed to do for the summer?" he asked.

"Here is the deal, Rob," I answered. "You have a permanent job offer starting next year on September 1. But it is contingent upon you spending next summer in New York City working one of two jobs: you can either work construction for three months, or you can drive a taxi for three months. With either of these jobs, I figure that you will lose the arrogance and sense of entitlement that you constantly display either by figuring it out on your own or when one of your coworkers physically beats it out of you. But however it happens, I win. You let me know what you decide."

"Who do you think you are?" Rob screamed. "God?"

"No," I said. "I'm the one with the job offers."

He stormed out of my office, never to return. Needless to say, he did not accept the job.

Three years later, in 1990, I received a phone call in my office. I certainly wasn't expecting this call, but it quickly became a cherished memory.

"Kurt, it's Rob Reese," the caller said.

"Rob, you old rapscallion," I said. "How in the hell are you?"

"I'm great," he said. "Do you remember the job offer you gave me the last time we were together, and the caveats that went with it?" he asked.

"I sure do," I answered.

"I just wanted you to know," he continued, "that it was the best professional advice I have ever received, and I wanted to thank you."

Blow me over with a feather. And give that man a Cohiba.

Prison Time

Recruiting is an important function for all companies—but it is critical at management consulting firms. Such firms are, quite literally, the sum of their people. They don't make products. They don't really provide services, in the sense that an architect or a CPA does. They try to help their clients solve problems or exploit opportunities. As one colleague suggested, "We're just brains on a stick."

Now I'm not sure that I'd go quite that far, but what good consultants do is pretty cerebral. They listen and gather facts. They analyze data and formulate hypotheses. They test hypotheses and draw conclusions. But usually the most important thing that a management consultant does is to define the client's problem: clearly, specifically, and unambiguously.

It always amazed me how quickly clients would leap to any old, convenient problem. They would do it based on instinct, surface information, and conventional wisdom.

"Our costs are too high," they would frequently say.

"Too high relative to what?" we would ask.

"They're just too high," the client would respond. "Our margins are too low, and we've got to cut costs."

Often, once we got into the company and their data, we would discover that they didn't have a cost problem at all; they had a pricing problem or a design problem or a utilization problem. Once we had clearly defined the problem, the remedies were usually pretty self-evident and the client could get to work solving the "real" problem. I would guess that a scenario like this, while admittedly more nuanced and complex, played out in 70 percent of the client assignments in which I was involved.

All of this is a long-winded way of saying that 100 percent of any management consulting firm's success and prosperity is due to the quality and talent of their partners and staff. They must be quick studies, able to get up to speed very rapidly in new companies and unfamiliar industries. They need to be able to think in analogies. They must be very analytical, curious, and articulate. And they must be team players. All of this is why recruiting is so fundamental to the success of any professional services firm, but particularly a management consulting firm.

There were a number of partners and staff who played an active role in recruiting every year. I was one of those folks. For starters, this required traveling to our business school alma maters to speak with the faculty and collect intelligence about the top performers in the program. This would happen long before the start of the official recruiting season.

Then we would visit the top schools and make presentations to interested students about both the profession and the firm. Such events hosted by all the blue-chip consulting firms—Booz Allen, McKinsey, Boston Consulting Group, Bain—were always very well attended.

I remember one time when my mentor and partner, Jack McGrath, and I were making such a presentation at Carnegie Mellon University in Pittsburgh. Jack and I were both alums of the CMU business school, so this presentation had special meaning to each of us. These were our peeps.

Both Jack and I had finished our individual remarks and were entertaining questions. A nice young lady in the front row stood up and asked, "Are the travel and work demands in management consulting as bad as we have been led to believe?"

Jack stepped forward. "Management consulting is a tough and demanding business," he said. "We do travel a lot. And we do put in the hours. But I have found that if you want to do something important in life, it always takes real commitment and real sacrifice. If you don't want to pay the price, I suggest that you go raise chickens in Iowa."

That left the audience a bit shell-shocked. They weren't used to such direct talk. They were used to being mollycoddled. It took them some time to gather themselves and reengage with questions. But I've always admired Jack for speaking the truth.

Then it came time for on-campus interviews. This usually happened in February and March of every year. Based on our review of the résumés of each student, as well as the faculty research conducted earlier in the year, we would invite some number of candidates to an interview. That might be six to eight at some schools or twenty to thirty at others. We would also have open schedules to allow other interested students to sign up for an interview on a first-come, first-served basis.

Each student would be interviewed by two Booz Allen professionals. One would conduct an achievement screen: Where has the candidate been successful in the past, and what do they aspire to do? Are they articulate? Do they get rattled easily?

The other would conduct an analytical screen: How smart is the candidate? How do they approach problem-solving? Do they try to dimension things with numbers? Are they logical?

I had one candidate tell me, several years after the fact, that his Booz Allen interview was "the most difficult two hours of my life." I don't know if they were that bad. But they were tough, and they were rigorous.

At the end of the day, the recruiting team would assemble to review the day's results. Only if, after being grilled by their colleagues, both interviewers were strongly supportive, would that candidate would be asked to visit a Booz Allen office for another round of interviews.

Then if there was 100 percent agreement among the eight or ten people who interviewed him or her during the office visit, including at least two or three partners, that candidate would finally receive an offer to join the firm upon graduation. It was a tough process. Only the best and the brightest made it through.

I used to particularly enjoy on-campus interviewing. It was always a grueling day. Conducting ten or twelve interviews of one hour each can really tucker you out. But it was a chance to meet some very interesting and talented people. It was also a chance to have a lot of laughs.

One tool that I used frequently in analytical screens was the Three-Minute Mystery. I would present a situation, and the candidate would be asked to figure out what was going on. They had three minutes to ask whatever questions they wanted.

Here is a real simple one to give you an idea about how they work:[1]

> Me: A man's very short conversation cost him a quarter, but he wasn't using a pay phone. Explain.

> Candidate: Did he pay someone to borrow their phone?

> Me: No.

> Candidate: Does the phone have anything to do with the answer?

---

[1] *Mind-Boggling One-Minute Mysteries and Brain Teasers*
© 2010 by Sandy Silverthorne and John Warner
Published by Harvest House Publishers
Eugene, Oregon 97402
www.harvesthousepublishers.com
Used by permission

Me: No.

Candidate: Did the man buy something with the quarter?

Me: No.

Candidate: Hmmm. You said it was a short conversation. Was it longer than a minute?

Me: No.

Candidate: Does the conversation have anything to do with the answer?

Me: Yes.

Candidate: Was the man angry or upset?

Me: Yes.

Candidate: Is this what the conversation was about?

Me: Yes.

Candidate: Was the quarter a coin?

Me: No.

Candidate: Was it a time period?

Me: Yes.

Candidate: Was the man a basketball player?

Me: Yes.

Candidate: Did this also involve the referee?

Me: Yes.

Candidate: Did someone get thrown out of the game?

Me: Yes. The player cussed out the ref at the end of the third quarter and got thrown out of the game, thus costing him the fourth quarter.

This is a somewhat simplistic example. But you get the idea. The point of these exercises was not to see if the candidate could get the right answer. In the example shown above, if the candidate knew the trick and gave the right answer immediately, I would have learned nothing. What these exercises allowed me to do was to get inside the head of the interviewee and take a peek at their wiring diagram: Can they think on their feet? Are their questions logical? Do they eliminate categories of possible answers? Do they lead somewhere promising? Can they think?

The other thing that I used to do in interviews was to ask candidates really off-the-wall questions to see if I could rattle them. Here are some questions that I used to use, followed by some actual winning and losing answers:

Me: You seem to be a smart fellow. So what's the smartest idea you ever had?

Candidate #1: I remember one time back in my undergraduate economics class, I … (I stopped listening at that point. He didn't get an offer.)

Candidate #2: The one I just made when I decided not to answer your question, no matter how much you badger me. (The word "badger" alone got him an offer, but he didn't take the job.)

Me: How do I tie my shoes?

Candidate #1: You take the laces, cross them, and make a knot. (Sorry, Charlie: no offer.)

Candidate #2: It's easy. You score exactly as many points as your shoes scored. That way you're tied. (He got an offer, and he took it.)

Me: Have you ever done time in prison?

Candidate #1: Absolutely not. That question was offensive. (He didn't get an offer.)

Candidate #2: Does one night in jail for a drunk and disorderly count? (She got an offer, accepted it, and was elected to the partnership six years later.)

I've got fond memories of these recruiting adventures. Plus I was able to hire some really terrific people, many of whom remain friends to this day.

Cough!

One of the responsibilities of the managing partner of an office at Booz Allen Hamilton was to hold regular staff meetings. The partners and staff were routinely traveling all over the country, and at times, all over the world. So keeping everyone up to date with information about the firm and about each other was a major challenge.

When I took over as managing partner of the Atlanta office in the late 1980s, I decided that monthly staff meetings were too frequent, so I scheduled them quarterly. I also thought there should be an important social aspect to these events, so I started them at 4:00 p.m. on Fridays, and followed them with a cocktail hour, and at times, a voluntary dinner.

Staff meetings usually covered a number of housekeeping items: new hires, promotions, anniversaries, birthdays, and such. I talked about the performance of the firm and about new, interesting client assignments that had recently been won. And I reviewed various policies and programs.

Finally, I gave the staff a chance to bring up any issues or concerns or ideas that they wanted to discuss. At one meeting, our receptionist, Ginny, raised the subject of charitable giving.

"Does the firm support any charities or other outreach programs?" she asked.

"Yes," I said. "I don't know the firm wide numbers, but last year the Atlanta office donated $25,000."

"Who decides where the money goes?" she continued.

"The partners generally decide what initiatives to support," I answered.

"Why do the partners get to decide?" she asked. "Shouldn't our charitable giving reflect the desires of the whole office, not just the views of a few partners?"

"Good idea," I responded. "Why don't you, Chris, and Coleen form a committee and brainstorm how our charitable giving ought to work, and then come back to all of us with a set of recommendations." As I said, Ginny was the office receptionist. Coleen was a secretary. And Chris was a senior associate on the client service staff. I knew that all three of them enjoyed the respect of their colleagues. And importantly, none of them was a partner.

At the next staff meeting, Ginny presented their recommendations: first, the entire office would elect a Contributions Committee of four people. Anyone was eligible. Then the committee would poll their colleagues, develop an overall giving strategy, and propose the initial recipients of our support. The initial budget would be $30,000 per year.

The staff was unanimously supportive of Ginny's proposal. In fact, she got a standing ovation and a few shout-outs that we should put her on the client staff. I called for an immediate election, and we located some pencils and paper.

"Vote for four of your colleagues to represent you on the newly formed Contributions Committee," I instructed, and everyone voted. After collecting the ballots, I asked one of my partners to count the votes. He returned ten minutes later and announced the four winners. It was the original three folks—Ginny, Coleen, and Chris—plus our graphic designer, Peggy. Not a partner in sight.

Then Chris stood and said to his fellow committee members, "I propose that we elect Ginny as our chairman. She's the one that got this ball rolling."

Coleen and Peggy both said, "I vote yes," and Ginny was elected chairman. Just like that. This entire process took maybe thirty minutes. And for the thirty staff members in the meeting, it was an aspirational and inspirational half hour.

At the next staff meeting, Ginny presented their plan: we would give money only to causes that we were willing to support with our time; we would limit donations to two causes, to achieve maximum impact; and we would support one cause related to the arts and one that supported children. This, she said, represented the consensus view of the entire office.

She said that the committee had selected the Atlanta Symphony Young Artists program, wherein we would underwrite one weekend concert during the season that featured an up-and-coming classical musician. And we would get personally involved by hosting a reception for the artist and inviting a number of business and community leaders to meet with him or her. As an aside, our first artist was now-famed violinist Midori, who was only sixteen years old when she performed with the Atlanta Symphony Orchestra.

The second cause that the committee proposed was CURE Childhood Cancer. This organization funded research into childhood cancer and led the fight to find a cure. But more important to our folks was their Patient and Family Services work. They ran something akin to a Ronald McDonald House that hosted family members when their children were in the hospital for treatment. They also had a number of support groups to help the kids and their parents cope with this horrible disease.

More important than our $15,000 per year in monetary support, the entire office really got involved with this organization. CURE offered us a seat on their board, and of course, we gave it to Ginny. Folks from the office baked cookies at least once a week for the kids and their parents. Each year, we hosted a big picnic at Stone Mountain for the kids, their parents, and their physicians and caregivers. By the third year, this picnic was nothing short of amazing. We got Coca-Cola to donate the use of one of their concession trailers and provide free soft drinks. We got other Atlanta-based companies to donate food and supplies. We got the Georgia Tech cheerleaders to make an appearance and put on a show. Some of our people dressed up as clowns. Some ran games for the kids. Others cooked burgers and hot dogs. We probably served two hundred people that year.

For a lot of our staff, this was the most rewarding day of the year; it provided an opportunity to give back in a way that really mattered. On the other hand, for many, the day was also the toughest one of the year. Watching these children just broke your heart. Some showed up in ambulances and on gurneys and had to remain connected to their IVs during the picnic. Lots of them were bald because of the effects of their chemotherapy. But they were kids, and for one afternoon, they could forget about their problems and just have fun.

The involvement of the Atlanta office staff in these outreach events probably did more for morale and team building than anything else that we did. They really brought the group together. And it's amazing to think that it all came out of a staff meeting where our receptionist, Ginny, simply asked, "Does the firm support any charities or other outreach programs?"

Without question the craziest staff meeting took place on Friday, October 13, 1989, four days after my fortieth birthday. We held the meeting and the subsequent reception at the Ritz-Carlton hotel in downtown Atlanta, just a block from our office. The staff meeting turned a little ugly as I had to announce a new policy that pretty much pissed off the entire client service staff.

One of the perks of working at Booz Allen was a long-standing policy of being allowed to fly first class. This was a much-appreciated benefit, particularly when you realize that most of the client staff took several flights every week. For example, at one point, I was Delta Airlines twenty-third best customer in the world.

But it seems that the managing partner of the US business thought we could save some money by changing the first-class air policy and requiring everyone to fly coach. And he had the support of most of the New York partners, one of whom who told me, "I rarely fly. The change doesn't affect me at all. And maybe I'll make a little more money."

Back to the staff meeting: The folks were ticked. They were threatening all sorts of things, like hiding their first-class upgrade fees somewhere in their expense reports. It took me a long time to calm them down and suggest that they didn't want to lose their integrity and risk losing their jobs over a stupid policy change.

At that time, Delta Airlines offered their frequent flyers first-class upgrades for $10, $20, or $30, depending on the duration of the flight. "Just pay for the upgrade yourself and don't worry about it," I counseled them. "It's just not a big deal. And if you can't afford the thirty bucks, come see me, and I'll give it to you out of my own pocket." That seemed to work.

We adjourned the meeting and moved on to the reception. I thought as we walked into the room that the staff needed a little bit of a blowout to get them out of their first-class funk. And boy did they get one.

I knew that several of my partners from other offices had been invited to the reception, as there was a plan to celebrate my fortieth birthday. I had begged my Atlanta partners not to do anything crazy or embarrassing and told them I just wanted to share a few drinks with my partners and the staff.

Things were going smoothly and I was into my third drink when I heard a commotion at the door. Into the room marched this big-chested, small-waisted blonde in a nurse's uniform that was about two sizes too small. And then she started coming my way. The staff could already smell blood.

She walked directly up to me and said, "Kurt, I'm Nurse Goodbody, here to give you your fortieth birthday physical exam. Please take off your clothes."

Now at this point, lots of thoughts went through my head. If I did nothing, I was going to be the brunt of fifteen minutes of sick and embarrassing humor. On the other hand, I was the managing partner of the office; I couldn't take off my clothes. But I had decided earlier that the staff needed a blowout tonight, hadn't I? What the hell, I thought, you only live once.

I set my drink down and slowly began to remove my clothes: first, my tie; then my shoes and socks; then my shirt; then, after pausing to reconsider, my slacks; then my undershirt. I was now down to my tighty-whities. The staff was going nuts, hooting and hollering and cheering me on. At that point, I decided that I had gone far enough. I was not going full commando in front of the staff. So I sat down in a chair and said, "I'm ready, Nurse Goodbody."

Before I continue with the story, I must admit to being confused about people's reaction to underwear. I've had this confusion for as long as I can remember. Most people seem to be relaxed and comfortable around other people in bathing suits, but people tend to freak out when they see others in their undies. Are boxers all that different from swimming trunks? How is a bikini different than a bra and panties? I'm as comfortable showing myself in my underwear as I am in my bathing suit. I guess that I'm just weird that way.

Back to Nurse Goodbody. She leaned over me, pretending to listen to my heart with her stethoscope, and whispered in my ear, "I've been doing this act for three years, and no one has ever taken their clothes off. I don't know what to do."

I whispered back, "Well, sweetie pie, you had better figure it out, because you're the one who is going to look stupid if you can't come up with something."

About that time, one of my dear friends and partners, Tom Jones—who had flown in from Cleveland for the party—began to chant: "Cough test! Cough test! Cough test!"

The rest of the staff started to chime in, and they shortened to chant to "Cough! Cough! Cough!"

Now I need to explain what was going here. When conducting a physical exam on a man, a doctor checks for a possible hernia by pushing his finger up into the patient's scrotum until he can feel his abdominal wall. He then has the patient turn his head and cough.

The pressure caused by the cough allows the doctor to feel any weakness in the abdominal wall. No weakness—no hernia.

So back to the party. Nurse Goodbody took my pulse and tested my reflexes. All the while, the staff was chanting for her to give me the hernia test: "Cough! Cough! Cough!" She had no idea what they were talking about until I whispered in her ear the way to perform a hernia test. She then turned beet red and said, "No way in hell!"

I knew the staff would keep up the chanting until we did something, so I whispered to Nurse Goodbody, "Trust me on this. Stand very close to me, put your arm between us and loudly say 'Cough!' We'll fake it."

She did as I asked, and I turned my head and coughed. The staff couldn't really see what was happening. But when I coughed, the cheers from the staff were deafening. And all thoughts of the new first-class air policy had evaporated.

Jules

L ife at Booz Allen Hamilton was fun, challenging, and rewarding. But it was also difficult. Many people felt they needed to work very long hours and six or even seven days a week just to keep up. Seventy-hour workweeks were common.

I had a different view. It was probably a result of being twenty-nine when I joined the firm and having had some fairly senior manufacturing management positions before I got there. This undoubtedly gave me some perspective and some self-confidence that I otherwise would have lacked.

During my first year with the firm, I had the opportunity to work on an interesting assignment led by Jim Wolf, a partner in the Cleveland office. We were trying to figure out a new distribution strategy for a major consumer products company, and the team was Jim, two senior client staff, and me, as the lowly green bean.

We were at the end of our second week of work and were having a team meeting in Jim's office on Friday afternoon to review our progress. Things were going great with the work. The analysis was coming together, and we were right on schedule.

Toward the end of the meeting, Jim said, "So tomorrow I think we should focus on inventory turnover."

"Tomorrow," I responded, "as in Saturday? Are you saying that you want us to work on Saturday?"

"Kurt, it is just common practice that we work for six or seven hours on Saturday unless someone has a conflict and can't do it."

"No one told me about weekend work when I was going through the interview process. And I'm not happy about. I'm willing to work twelve or fourteen hours a day during the week. And I'm willing to work weekends if we are behind schedule or facing a deadline. But I'm not working Saturday just to be working."

"Well damn, Kurt," Jim replied. "If you feel that strongly about it, I guess we can pick it up on Monday."

"Thanks, Jim. That sounds pretty good to me."

This whole issue of working weekends became something of a cause célèbre with me. I steadfastly refused to work weekends unless (1) the client had rescheduled a meeting or (2) the team had fallen behind schedule. I'm proud to say that over my first two years with the firm, I worked during all or part of only four weekends. I think that this was as much an attitude as anything else. I had colleagues that decided on Monday that they were going to have to work Saturday. I refused to give in until Friday afternoon. It's surprising how many rabbits you can pull out of your hat if you don't give up too early.

When I became a partner, I became even more strident. I refused to promote staff members who could not get their work done between Monday and Friday. My rational was simply this: if they had no time to recharge, the staff would eventually burn themselves out and would leave the firm. When that happened, all the time, money, and opportunity that I and others had invested in their development would go down the drain.

Some of the staff got really pissed off about this philosophy of mine. I remember that Bob Morin was considered by the Regional Appraisal Committee for promotion two years after joining the firm. The committee, which I happened to chair, recommended that Bob be immediately promoted to senior associate.

The following week, I reviewed his written appraisal with Bob and told him of the committee's recommendation. However, I said that I was not going to take the committees' advice and was delaying his promotion until he proved to me that he could get the work done without working every weekend.

"Bob," I said, "you do great work, and you have done an outstanding job. You are dedicated and respected and a leader. But, it frankly takes you too long to do it. You're in the office every Saturday and most Sundays. You will undoubtedly burn yourself out, and then you are of no value to either me or the firm. When you can look me in the eye and say 'I haven't worked a weekend in four months,' I will immediately promote you. And I'll make your salary increase retroactive."

"You son of a bitch," Bob replied. "Who do you think you are, God? It's my business when I work, not yours."

Bob stormed out of my office, devastated by my decision. Within a week, he was happy again, but he was starting to work smarter. Four months later, he walked into my office and proclaimed that he had not work a weekend in four months. I shook his hand, congratulated him, and promoted him on the spot.

Unfortunately, Bob still found a way to burn himself out, and he left the firm two years later. The good news is we remain friends to this day.

As I said at the start of this chapter, life at Booz Allen Hamilton was a challenge. Most of the time, this was a result of the work itself or the extensive travel required or of the need to always be "on."

Sometimes, however, the challenge was circumstantial, meaning that something or somebody put you into a situation that was difficult, maybe even impossible, through no fault of your own. That happened to me on several occasions.

The best example occurred in 1979, during my first year with the firm. Johnny Diddel was the partner-in-charge of an assignment for a company in Minneapolis. It has been so long ago that I can't remember which company, but 3M comes to mind. I do know that the assignment involved a set of issues having to do with procurement, inventory management, and distribution. Booz Allen was, at that time, the best there was at supply chain management.

In addition to Johnny and me, the team included Ronnie Stevens and Bob Busker, both of whom were more senior than me. Being the most junior staff member on the team brought with it certain responsibilities and expectations, but nothing in the way of perks, rewards, or even gratitude.

The junior person usually wrote the first draft of client reports, only to have them ripped to shreds by their seniors. The lowest one in the pecking order usually had to shepherd reports and other documents through production and proofread them for accuracy. Typos were never the fault of the typist; they were the fault of the junior associate on the team. I'm not whining. That's just the way things were—sort of a rite of passage.

One Tuesday, we were in the office preparing our first progress report for the client. The progress meeting was scheduled for Wednesday at 8:00 a.m. in the client's Minneapolis offices. And we had airline reservations on the last flight on Tuesday from Cleveland to Minneapolis, which departed at 7:30 p.m. from Cleveland Hopkins Airport.

Things were moving along pretty well Tuesday morning. We were drafting and editing and redrafting the presentation, and it was beginning to come together pretty nicely. That is until Mr. Diddel read the report for the first time at about one thirty.

"This is crap!" he proclaimed. "Tear it up and start over." Johnny was not happy.

We dove in and started rethinking and rewriting the presentation. By four o'clock, we had finally seen the light about what we had screwed up and were dutifully writing a different story. By five o'clock, we had a good working draft and gave it to Johnny to review.

"It is getting better," he declared. "But it still has a long way to go. Give me an hour, and I'll write the damn thing myself."

We had been watching the clock for some time. It was now five. Johnny needed until six. Then we had to get a fifty-page presentation retyped, proofread, copied, and bound. Our flight was scheduled for 7:30 p.m., and we were a half hour from the airport. Oh mama!

Mr. Diddel finished up a little after six o'clock, and the result was stellar. I guess that was the reason he was a partner. The secretaries, graphic artists, and production people were hard at work, but it looked like we were going to miss our deadline.

Johnny called me into his office, closed the door, and said, "Kurt, our flight is scheduled for 7:30 p.m., and it is your job to be sure that we are on that plane. Do whatever you need to do, but don't let that plane leave without us. Am I clear?"

"Yes, sir," I answered as I left his office without a clue as to what to do.

The first thing I decided was to have two cabs downstairs at 6:30 so whenever we were ready to go, transportation would be available. I went downstairs at 6:40 to ensure the cabs had arrived. They had, and I gave each cab driver $20 and told them I would triple the fare to the airport if they would wait for us.

Then I went back upstairs to the office to formulate my strategy. I checked with the production people, and they told me that the reports would be boxed up and ready to go by 7:15 tops. That implied the following schedule: leave at 7:15, cabs by 7:17, airport by 7:42 and the gate by 7:50. I had to get them to hold the flight for at least twenty minutes, assuming I could get everything to work like clockwork.

So then I started thinking about how I could get the airline to hold the plane for twenty minutes or so. Maybe I could call them and claim to be the county sheriff: "I have a prisoner that has to be extradited to Minneapolis. The prisoner is scheduled to appear before a Federal judge at nine o'clock tomorrow morning, and your Minneapolis flight this evening is the only way to get him there. The prisoner is being processed right now and could be driven straight up to the plane. I think that I could have him there with a Federal marshal before eight o'clock. Can you hold the plane?"

Then I thought that it might be better to claim to be a maintenance supervisor with the airline in Minneapolis: "I have a problem. We have a fully booked 747 flight tomorrow morning from Minneapolis. I just learned that the aircraft has a mechanical problem, and the flight will have to be canceled unless I can get a replacement part here tonight. The only spare part I could find was in Columbus, so I arranged for someone to drive it to Cleveland an hour ago. Unfortunately, the driver is stuck in traffic. He estimates he will arrive between 7:45 and 8:00. Can you hold the plane?"

I ended up going with my third idea, which had a nice life-and-death aspect to it. I looked up Northwest Airlines in the phone book and found a number that said Hopkins Airport Operations. At exactly 7:10, I called them, and here is what I said:

"My name is Bill Anderson, and I am calling on behalf of Doctor Jules Irving from the Cleveland Clinic. Dr. Irving is a world-class heart surgeon specializing in myocardial valve replacement, and he has just been called by the Mayo Clinic in Rochester, Minnesota, and asked to assist in a complicated surgery that they have scheduled for seven o'clock tomorrow morning. I have an open ticket for Dr. Irving, but I would appreciate it if you could make him a reservation on your 7:30 flight to Minneapolis. And here is the hard part: Dr. Irving is just now finishing up in the OR here. I have arranged for a police escort to take him to the airport, but it doesn't look like he will make it until 7:50. Can you hold the plane for him?" I held my breath.

"Have him come to the departures level at Terminal B. I will meet him in a cart and take him directly to the gate. My name is Kirby Green. Call me back at this number if you need anything."

The reports weren't boxed and ready to go until 7:20. As we got into the cab, Johnny asked me, "Are we going to make the plane?"

"Guaranteed," I answered confidently.

The cabs pulled up to the airport at 7:45. We sprinted through the airport and arrived at the gate at 7:50, precisely as I had planned. The lounge was empty, but the plane was still there and the door was still open. We hurried to the gate, presented our tickets, and boarded. Our first-class seats were waiting for us. After a few minutes, Mr. Diddel asked the flight attendant, "What seems to be the holdup?"

"We're waiting for a surgeon from the Cleveland Clinic. He should be here shortly." Johnny turned and gave me a smile.

A few minutes later, they closed the door and we taxied away from the gate. "What happened to the surgeon?" Johnny asked.

"I don't know," she said. "Apparently, the Cleveland Clinic has never heard of anyone named Dr. Jules Irving."

Johnny looked over at me and gave me a wink and a smile. Nothing more was ever said.

Crazy Days

Follow the words of Hunter S. Thompson: Life should not be a journey to the grave with the intention of arriving safely in a pretty and well-preserved body, but rather to skid in broadside in a cloud of smoke, thoroughly used up, totally worn out, and loudly proclaiming, "Wow! What a ride!"

Hail Sneezer

It has been my experience that most doctors and dentists have an undeveloped sense of humor. It's as if they were so absorbed in learning body parts that they didn't have time to hone their wit. In fact, they didn't even have time to learn to appreciate wit.

I'm sure you've seen it. You tell your doctor or dentist a really funny joke, and they just don't get it. When you give them the punch line, they don't laugh; they don't even smile. They just look at you with glazed eyes and respond "Okay," as if to say "Go on" or "And then what happened?" They miss it completely. And worse, they don't seem to care if they miss it.

I've been fortunate to have had some funny doctors and dentists, and I've had more than a few funny stories take place in their offices. I know that these are rare occurrences, but that's what makes them all the more enjoyable.

When we lived in Greenwich, Connecticut, I had a world-class dentist named Richard Redville. He taught part-time at Columbia University and was a recognized expert in certain aspects of general dentistry. He was also a very good guy. We shared a lot of laughs when I was in his chair.

I remember one time when he was recommending that I have some reconstructive work done. I'd had some crowns put in maybe twenty years earlier, and he thought it was time to replace them.

"So you really think we should do this?" I asked.

"Yes," he said. "I think it's time."

"Why now?" I pushed. "Why not later?"

"Because Porsche just came out with that new 911C Turbo, and I've just got to have one. Have you seen how much those babies cost?"

"Are you nuts?"

"Don't worry," he said. "I was just pulling your leg. You're going to need to replace them in the next few years. But you can do it now or do it later."

"Later," I answered.

It was great to have a dentist with a sense of humor. He also drove very nice cars. But I do remember getting even with him at a later appointment.

Have you ever noticed those "prompt payment" reminder signs in your doctor's or dentist's office? Richard's waiting room sign said: "Payment Is Expected *as* Service Is Rendered."

I was back in his chair some time later, and I had put a wad of fifty-dollar bills in my pants pocket. About ten minutes into the procedure, I motioned for him to stop as I wanted to say something. I reached in my pocket and pulled out a fifty.

"Here," I said, handing him the money.

"What's this?" Richard asked.

"I'm just following the rules, Doc."

"What are you talking about?"

"The rule on the sign in your waiting room," I said.

"I have no idea what you are talking about," Richard said, dumbfounded.

"In your waiting room, you posted a sign that says, and I quote, 'Payment Is Expected as Service Is Rendered.' It doesn't say 'after service is rendered.' It doesn't say 'before you leave.' It says, clear as day, '*as* service is rendered.' I'm just trying to follow your rules."

"Okay by me," he said as he put the fifty in his pocket and went back to work. Unfortunately, after giving him $300 in fifties, one every ten minutes for an hour, I still had a bill for $429.50 when I checked out. I guess he had the last laugh after all.

In the 1980s, we lived in Atlanta. My doctor was a great guy named Peter Rayburn. He was a top-notch physician, who had studied at Harvard Medical School. In maybe 1984, I was having my annual physical exam. During the exam, I asked him about a sneezing problem that I had been experiencing for some time.

"Peter," I reported, "when I sneeze, I usually keep on sneezing for some time."

"Tell me more," he said.

"Well," I continued, "if I sneeze once, I usually sneeze at least fifty times."

"What do you think is causing it?" he asked.

"My hypothesis is that when I sneeze once, the sneeze irritates my nasal passages. That irritation causes me to sneeze again. This irritates my nasal passages even more, which causes me to sneeze again. This vicious cycle continues until the nerve endings in my nose become numb, at which point I stop sneezing."

Said Dr. Peter Rayburn, highly respected physician and graduate of the Harvard School of Medicine: "That's probably a better explanation than anything I could come up with."

Snake, Snake, Fly

Let's just say that I've known a few snakes in my time. The first one that comes to mind is a former client from San Diego. This snake is very well-known in business, social, and philanthropic circles, so I can't use his real name. Let's call him Wilbur Too Slick. Wilbur was the CEO of a big Fortune 500 company. And he has given away billions to very good causes. That said, I'm a bit cynical. I know firsthand that he is an egotist of the highest order. And he is into power and control. Lots of business executives fit this mold, but Wilbur was the poster child.

In 1991, his company was having some serious performance problems in their operations. Let's call them Viper Industries. At the time, I was the service operations practice leader at Booz Allen, and so I was the natural one to respond when Wilbur asked us for help.

I flew to San Diego and met with Mr. Too Slick for several hours. His personality was a little grating, and he struck me as a bit of a self-centered jerk; but I had worked with similar folks before, and it was no big deal. I returned to New York and wrote a proposal for how Booz Allen would help him fix his problems and then flew to San Diego again to present our proposal to him.

On this trip, he warmed up considerably and was enthusiastic when he said that after reviewing several other proposals, he was awarding the work to us. We were, he said, more experienced and more qualified than the other major firms to whom he had spoken. I was growing fonder of Wilbur by the minute.

The assignment was a major one for the firm. As I recall, I had priced the first phase at $750,000. I assigned five client service staff members to the work and estimated that it would take three months to complete. I also thought that our involvement would likely be required for a year or so after that to assist in implementing the suggested restructuring, and I told that to Mr. Too Slick upfront.

We had been working on the assignment for two weeks when I took the staff out for a well-deserved team dinner. They had been busting their butt, and things were going very well with the client. After dinner, I retired to the hotel bar for a nightcap and some alone time. I wound up sitting next to a guy about my age—let's call him Brad—and we struck up a conversation.

At some point, I asked him what he did.

"I'm a management consultant," he answered.

"You're kidding," I replied. "I am too."

"Yeah, I'm a partner with McKinsey out of Chicago."

"I'll be damned. I'm a partner with Booz Allen in New York."

"Are you out here on client work?" he asked.

"Yes, I'm leading an assignment for a company just a couple of blocks away."

"How ironic," Brad said. "So am I."

This was beginning to get eerie. "Is it north or south of here?" I asked.

"North."

"I shouldn't ask this, but is it Viper Industries?"

"Yes, it is," he said.

We went on talking. After about fifteen minutes, it became obvious that good old Wilbur had hired McKinsey & Company to do the same exact work as we had been retained to do. All of his comments about our experience and qualifications distinguishing us from our competitors were a bunch of bull. Mr. Too Slick wanted to have a bake-off, meaning that two of us would do the same assignment and the one who did it the best would get the $2–$3 million of follow-on work.

Now I don't have anything against a bake-off. I love competition as much as the next guy. And not to toot my own horn, but over my twenty-five-year consulting career, I never lost a competitive assignment to McKinsey & Company. I would have been happy to have participated in a bake-off, if only Wilbur had told me—and Brad—upfront.

The essence of any professional services relationship is mutual trust. It applies to all such providers: doctors, lawyers, consultants, accountants. The client must trust the provider to offer honest, informed counsel. And the provider must trust the client to tell the truth—all the time. This is the only way such a professional relationship can work.

I told Brad, "I have good news for you. At eight o'clock tomorrow morning, I am resigning from this assignment. I can't work for a client that plays games behind my back. To hell with him—it's all yours. Good luck with Too Slick."

Brad said that were it up to him, he would resign too. Unfortunately, he was a junior partner and could not make this decision on his own. He said he was going back to his room to make some calls. I have no idea what McKinsey decided to do, but I hope that they also told old Wilbur Too Slick to stick it.

At precisely eight o'clock the next morning, I showed up at Wilbur's office. "I'm sorry, Kurt, but I have meetings scheduled nonstop all morning. Can we speak this afternoon?" he asked.

"This will only take a minute."

"Okay."

"Wilbur, last night I think I learned that you hired McKinsey & Company to do the same exact assignment that you hired us to do—sort of a bake-off for the next phase of work. Is that true?" I asked.

"Well, Kurt, so what if I did? It's my company."

"Wilbur, I've got late-breaking news: McKinsey wins the bake-off, because we resign. Your behavior has to be one of the sleaziest things a client has ever done to me. And even worse, you were willing to piss a million dollars of your stockholder's money down the drain just to play your little game. I'll send you an invoice for our time and expenses to date. And I strongly, make that very strongly, suggest that you pay it promptly."

I went down to our team room and announced that we were through at Viper and that everyone should go back to the hotel, pack up, and catch the next flight home. And since it was Thursday, I told them to take Friday off and have some fun.

By the time I got back to the New York office, the story was already out. And apparently Wilbur had called a couple of senior partners that he knew and demanded my head. One in particular, Joe Nathan, was furious and claimed that I had called a valued client a sleazeball.

"He is a sleazeball, Joe," I said. "But I didn't call him that. I accused him of sleazy behavior, and of that, he is 100 percent guilty. He is a snake, pure and simple. And by the way, if you are going to demand that I be fired, ask our colleagues which of us they would rather have as a partner, me or the snake? I'll take my chances."

I never heard another word about it, although it was added to the lore of the firm. And good old Wilbur paid my invoice in full.

Snakes like Wilbur, I can deal with. They always shoot themselves in the end. Real snakes are another matter. I am petrified of these creatures. I know that my fear is not rational, but I just can't help it. The mere sight of a snake on TV can sometimes cause me to have nightmares.

In 1984, I invited my client Jim Meyer, CEO of a large aluminum cable company, to play golf at my club. It was midmorning, and Jim was driving the cart when up ahead I saw a big black snake crossing the cart path. This bad boy was maybe twenty feet in front of us.

"Please stop the cart right now," I said to Jim in a no-nonsense manner and with a decided sense of urgency.

He stopped right away, and I continued, "Jim, in what I am about to say, I am as serious as a heart attack. Do not make fun. Do not get cute. Or I will take a sand wedge out of my bag and beat you to death. Now, there is a very big black snake crossing the cart path up ahead of us. I want to sit very still right where we are until he disappears into the bushes. Then I want to count slowly to two hundred to be sure that it doesn't decide to turn around and come back. Then we can resume our cart ride."

Jim must have sensed my utter desperation because all he said was "No problem." We waited for four or five minutes and then proceeded on to the next tee. Jim never said a word about the experience. What a friend.

•••◆━━━━━◆━━━━━◆•••

My scariest experience with a snake took place in Pittsburgh, where I was going to graduate school in 1977. It was a Saturday morning, and I was home in our apartment in Squirrel Hill. One of my roommates, Jim Bachman, was there as well. After breakfast, I went into the bathroom for my morning constitutional. I took along a *Reader's Digest* to keep me occupied, and after assuming the throne, I opened it up.

I turned to an article about Morocco and started to read. At one point the author took up the subject of the king cobra, a lethal snake indigenous to the area. There were some hikers who, unbeknownst to them, were bearing down on a nest of cobras.

In the next paragraph, just as the hikers were about to step into the nest, one of the cobras coiled, getting ready to strike. At exactly that moment, as I was reading that passage, a housefly decided to land on my right buttock. Convinced that I had just been bitten by a king cobra, I screamed at the top of my lungs and literally jettisoned myself off the commode. I ended up in the bathtub gasping for air.

My friend Jim yelled to me: "Are you alright?"

"I think I might just live. But the fly must die!"

Birdie

The cruise line industry is a decidedly fixed cost operation. The ship, the fuel, and the officers and crew expenses are the same regardless of how many passengers take any particular cruise. About the only variable expense is the cost of the groceries. And midnight buffets notwithstanding, food costs are surprisingly low. If memory serves me correctly, when a cruise line sells over 92 percent of its available capacity, they print money. But if less than 85 percent of the cabins are occupied, they lose their keister.

In the mid-1980s, there was a relatively mild recession in the United States. Lots of folks cut back on their discretionary spending, and no surprise, that included Caribbean cruise vacations. As demand for cruises fell, one competitor, Carnival Cruise Line, decided to take decisive action. In an effort to fill up their ships, they announced that they would offer free airfare from anywhere in the United States to anyone booking a cruise on Carnival. Of course, all of Carnival's competitors had no choice but to quickly follow suit.

Many people thought that Carnival was nuts, because once their competitors all followed their lead, they would gain no relative advantage. They would simply give away a lot of money. I always thought that Carnival was dumb like a fox. They were in a much stronger marketing and financial position to absorb the new expense. And I'm sure they saw the boom in demand for cruises that free airfare would create once the recession was over. Whether they were prescient or just lucky, their strategy worked. Carnival added eight cruise ships to its five-ship fleet from 1992 through 1999 and emerged as the unchallenged industry leader.

The announcement of free airfare caused havoc for most competitors. One such company was Norwegian Cruise Line, or as it was known in 1983, Norwegian Caribbean Line. NCL's CEO, Rob Feller, requested proposals from several management consulting firms to help the company deal with the issue. I led the team from Booz Allen Hamilton, and we were fortunate that Rob selected us to do the work. The issue was pretty clear. Prior to free airfare, NCL had annual revenues of about $250 million and made about $35 million in profit. Free airfare cost them about $65 million per year. Overnight, this expense went from nonexistent to the largest single line item in their budget. Whew! NCL went from making $35 million a year to losing $30 million a year—all in an instant.

We spent about two years working on a wide variety of assignments for NCL. We got involved in everything from marketing to pricing to operations, and from revenue enhancement to cost reduction. I'm proud to report that they returned to profitability within eighteen months, and continued to grow their profits every year thereafter. It was a great client/consultant partnership.

One of the necessities of leading all this work was I had to spend a lot of time on the cruise ships. After all, they *were* the product and they *were* where all the money was made and spent. In all, I was on twenty-one different cruises over a two-year period—some for a week, some for three days. I didn't get much sympathy either at home or in the office for all the hard work that my team and I were doing. But believe me, twelve and fourteen hour days of real work were the norm.

I became very good friends with one of the captains, Lars Halversen, and that is where this story begins. Lars drove the ship on at least ten of the cruises that I took. He was a very accomplished captain and was very helpful to us in doing our work. But when the work was done, he was funny and sociable and a bit of a prankster. He always invited me to sit with him at the Captain's Gala Black-Tie

Dinner, which occurred on one night of every cruise; that is the night that the passengers can get their picture taken with the captain.

At every dinner, Lars would try to convince me to become an honorary Viking. All I needed to do to have this title bestowed upon me was to drink one full bottle of aquavit during an evening. For those of you who don't know, aquavit is the national drink of Norway. Here is a condensed version of what Wikipedia has to say about it:

> Aquavit is an important part of Norwegian drinking culture, where it is often drunk during festive gatherings. Aquavit is made from potatoes and is matured in oak casks. Then the drink is served at room temperature in tulip-shaped glasses. Aquavit arguably complements dark beer well, and its consumption is very often preceded by a swig of beer. But purists generally lament this practice, claiming the beer will ruin the flavor and aftertaste. This practice is mainly seen among younger Norwegians, who wish to carry on the tradition of toasting in aquavit at festive occasions, but are not particularly fond of the bitter taste and high level of alcohol.

Every time Lars brought this up, I told him that he was nuts. I had no intention of drinking an entire bottle of aquavit, and I had no desire to become a Viking. My refusal worked on several occasions, but it failed me on one memorable night. It began after the captain's dinner, when Lars began ordering after-dinner aquavits for all seven of his table guests. He then proposed a toast, after which everyone downed their shot and shouted "Skol!" After about three drinks, I told Lars that I'd had enough. In a stern voice, he told me quietly not to embarrass him in front of his guests. So I continued toasting. He was, after all, my client.

I have very few memories of anything that followed, but apparently, I joined in a couple more toasts at the table. Then Lars and I and a couple of senior officers adjourned to the bar. There I consumed shot after shot of the dreaded aquavit. When I asked him later if I had drunk a whole bottle, Lars smiled and said I had drunk much more than one bottle.

At some point, I apparently decided it would be a good idea to try my luck at blackjack. Prankster Lars willingly showed me to the tables. I was later told that I bought $100 in chips and proceeded to play. I must have reasoned that I needed to hit twenty-one exactly to assure a win, because I apparently took another card whenever I had any count less than twenty-one. Of course, my $100 was gone within minutes.

That is when Lars apparently stepped in. He asked for the pit boss and read him the riot act for allowing such an obviously inebriated person to gamble. He said he would close down the casino for the duration of the cruise if he didn't immediately return my money. The pit boss couldn't pay me quick enough. It's good to have friends in high places.

I was then put to bed in my cabin, which was in the officer's quarters, next door to Lars. I was awakened the next morning by Lars' Korean room steward, Mr. Oh.

"Oh God, Oh," I said. "What the hell happened to me?"

"The captain said that you had tough night but that you need to get up right now. You and the captain play golf today. He said that he will be here in ten minutes. Take a shower, drink coffee and pull yourself together," Oh ordered.

The next thing I knew I was on a boat being tendered ashore from the ship, which was anchored offshore, to Cozumel, Mexico. Lars and I were going to play the first officer and the chief engineer in an eighteen-hole golf match. We got to shore, hopped in a cab, went to the golf course, rented clubs, and proceeded to the first tee.

The first hole was a par four with a 90° dogleg to the left. If you played the hole properly, you would hit your drive maybe 250 yards straight off the tee. You would then hit an iron shot straight to the left for about 150 yards onto the green. Being the captain, Lars had honors. Wanting to forestall the inevitable for as long as possible, I teed off last. The other three guys hit their drives right down the middle and were all in good shape. Then it was my turn.

As I approached the ball, I had trouble focusing. My partner, Lars, came to the rescue by saying, "Kurt, I know you're seeing three balls. Just aim for the middle one."

I let it rip and hooked the ball hard to the left. It bounded over a fence and landed in the swimming pool of a house neighboring the golf course. "Damn it!" I said.

I jumped the fence, retrieved the ball from the pool, took a drop in the neighbor's backyard, and grabbed my trusty six iron. Then I took a nice, relaxed swing, aiming once again for the middle ball. Up it went, landing just in front of the green. Three bounces and a twenty-foot roll and, yes, into the cup. One off the tee, one out of the water, one into the cup: Birdie three!

Lars and I went on to win the match. And the intense heat of the Mexican sun literally baked the hangover right out of me. When we got back to the ship, my colleagues—eyewitnesses to the prior evening's festivities—were amazed that I was even standing, let alone feeling just great. Thanks, Mom and Dad, for the strong constitution; it comes in handy every once in a while.

Later I asked Lars how in the hell he was able to drink all of those shots of aquavit at dinner and still function. "Aquavit?" he said. "I don't drink that stuff. It'll kill you. I have my waiter bring me brown tea in a tulip glass. Gotcha!"

War Zone

I've been fortunate to have had season tickets to a number of football, basketball, and baseball games, be they college or pro. I grew up in Columbus, Ohio, and had season football tickets for the Ohio State Buckeyes from 1971 to 1974. Ohio State won or tied for the Big Ten Championship in three of those years. And I was there to see it all.

When Bonita and I lived in Cleveland from 1979 to 1981, I had access to good season tickets to see my beloved Cleveland Browns. That was the time of Brian Sipe and the Kardiac Kids, who put the Brownies back into contention. The best game I ever saw was on January 4, 1981, when they played host to the Oakland Raiders in an AFC divisional play-off game.

It was cold as hell that Sunday in Cleveland; in fact, it was reported that with the wind-chill factor, the temperature at game time was thirty-five below zero. That didn't stop the loyal Browns fans. Many were running through the stands during the game, stripped to the waist, cheering for a Cleveland victory. We really thought that this might be the year for the Brownies to go to the Super Bowl.

The Browns were down 14–12 with two minutes and twenty-two seconds remaining in the game when they took possession of the ball at their own fifteen-yard line. They methodically drove the ball down the field, seemingly immune to the cold. With forty-nine seconds to go, they had moved the ball down to the Raiders' nine-yard line and only needed a chip-shot field goal to win the game. Instead of kicking the gimme field goal and running out the clock to win the game, the Browns decided to try one more play for a touchdown. Why they decided this is anyone's guess. If they had gone up 15–14, they would have most certainly won the game. The Raiders were not going to march the ball down the field and score in less than thirty seconds in sub-zero weather.

So what happened? Brian Sipe threw an interception to Raiders safety Mike Davis in the end zone. Game over. The Brownies were foiled again. And all because Coach Sam Rutigliano overthought the situation and called a bonehead play. Oh, to have do-overs in Cleveland Stadium.

When we moved to Atlanta, we acquired some great forty-yard line season football tickets to the Georgia Bulldogs. We watched them win the SEC Championship while Herschel Walker won the Heisman Trophy in 1982. It was an exciting time. Then we opted for Georgia Tech football tickets for a few years in the mid-1980s. Fun times there too.

In 1984, I was able to get my hands on two season tickets to the Hawks, Atlanta's NBA basketball team. The seats were twelve rows up behind the Hawks bench. We saw lots of great basketball and lots of great players over the next eight years: Dominique Wilkins, Kevin Willis, Moses Malone, Spud Webb, Michael Jordan, Larry Bird, and Magic Johnson. What a time in the NBA.

Then we moved to New York. Yankee tickets were the top priority, and my buddy Frank Varasano and I pulled that off pretty quickly.

But the New York Giants were a different story. For the first couple of years that we lived in Greenwich, I got tickets for a few games each season from a ticket broker. That was okay, but the seats were usually mediocre and always in a different location. That began to get old.

Then, in 1994, I game across a guy who was selling his four season tickets on the fifty-yard line in row G, seven rows up from the field. These tickets had been in his family for years and had been passed down to him upon his father's death.

I don't remember his name, but let's call him Mel Tickets. He had two small children and was not a wealthy man. He couldn't really afford the tickets for himself, as the price was about $3,000 per season. So Mel decided to go ahead and buy them, use the tickets for the two preseason games for himself, and then sell the tickets for the eight regular-season games for double their face value and deposit that money into his children's college fund. I thought Mel had a good and noble idea, and I was happy to contribute. And fifty-yard line seats—come on. I bought his tickets for the next eight years.

The most memorable game that I ever attended at the Meadowlands was the Giants versus the Chargers game on December 23, 1995. My good friends Frank Varasano, Frank Jones, and Larry Roth joined me at the game.

New York City had received about twelve inches of snow a couple of days before the game. And for some reason, the Giants' grounds crew removed only some of the snow from the stands before the game. By game time Saturday, the aisles and the seats had been cleared, but much snow remained under the seats.

As you would expect, there were a few snowballs flying around from one stadium section to another during the first half of the game. But it was no big deal. However, in the second half, as the Giants squandered a 17–0 lead, the fans began to get a little rowdy. Before you knew it, Giant Stadium was engaged in an all-out snowball fight. Most of the action was between the fans in various parts of the stadium. Snowballs were flying everywhere.

Occasionally, one would be launched toward the field. I could understand the coaches and the refs being somewhat concerned. But even the players were getting jumpy. I found it hysterical that these manly, six-foot-eight, three hundred–pound players—with helmets and shoulder pads and rib pads and hip pads and knee pads and arm pads and face masks—would be nervous about a snowball fight. But they began to congregate in the center of the field to get out of the range of the incoming snowballs.

About that time, I noticed the Giants' coach, Dan Reeves, was standing on the sideline about thirty feet in front of me. Remember that I was just seven rows up from the field. I knew that I could hit Coach Reeves with just one shot. I made a perfect snowball and took aim. Just as I was ready to let it fly, my friend and partner Frank Jones, leaned over and put his arm out to stop me.

"Don't do it," Frank said. "You'll be the one that gets in trouble."

I heeded Frank's warning and let the snowball fly toward the upper deck. Little did I know at the time, but Frank had saved my bacon; more on this later.

The refs briefly cleared the field, and the snowball fight played itself out. The players returned, the game resumed, and, of course, the Giants lost to the Chargers 27–17 and ended the season with a 5–11 record.

It had been a dull and difficult game to watch for a Giants' fan. But the snowball fight had been memorable. It was a throwback to childhood. Fifty thousand fans heaving snowballs at one another like they were twelve years old. What a gas!

We walked through the parking lot to our car. Once we got in and got into the line of traffic trying to get out of the stadium, we turned on the radio to listen to the postgame report.

"They were animals," one announcer said. "I've never seen anything like it."

"Total disregard for human safety," said another. "They were putting lives at risk and didn't even care."

"The Giants organization should have cleared the snow before the game," an announcer added. "That was sheer negligence on their part. They should have seen this coming."

We were dumbfounded. These idiots were taking about the joyous snowball fight that we had just witnessed and participated in. What had we missed?

"I'm telling you," another said. "It was a war zone out there. I've never seen anything like it."

This kind of talk continued for fifteen or twenty minutes: how horrible the snowball fight had been; how the participants had put the players, coaches, and refs in harm's way (even though 95 percent of the action had been fan-to-fan); and what animals we were.

The next week, the newspapers picked up where the radio announcers had left off. They chastised the fans and criticized the Giants. Here is an excerpt from the *New York Times* of December 26, 1995. It was written by sportswriter Dave Anderson:

> When the snowball throwing continued, the referee Ron Blum threatened to declare a forfeit. He did not, but Wellington Mara, a Giants owner, said later that Blum "would have been justified" to rule a forfeit. The Giants later took a full-page ad in a San Diego newspaper apologizing for the "snowball game."
>
> Some 175 spectators were ejected and their tickets confiscated; 15 were arrested. Jeffrey Lange, 26, of Bridgewater, N.J., identified by a widely published photograph showing him throwing a snowball, was later arrested and charged with disorderly conduct. He was convicted of improper behavior and fined $650.

Mr. Lange also was forced to give up his fifty-yard line season tickets. But the eerie part was that Mr. Lange was seated in the same section as I, only about six rows behind me. And he let the snowball fly at almost the same time that I was prepared to nail Coach Reeves. Remember that I said that my pal Frank Jones had stopped me. It looks like he could well have been right and that he really did save my bacon ... and my tickets.

146

Let's Dance

I've probably served on at least fifteen boards of directors over the past twenty years. Some were multibillion-dollar public companies; some were small public companies; some were small, private start-up companies; some were not-for-profit companies; and some were charitable organizations. When it comes to governing boards, I've seen a thing or two.

One of the most fun boards that I served on was The Acting Company. I was on their board for seven years, from 2001 to 2007, and I served as chairman of the Finance Committee for most of that time.

The Acting Company is a not-for-profit theater repertory company. It was founded in 1972 by the famed British actor John Houseman and big-time theater insider Margot Harley. At that time, both John and Margot were professors in the Drama Division of the Juilliard School in New York, which admitted its first class in 1968. In 1972, the first class was about to graduate.

This class included such future stars as Kevin Kline, who went on to appear in movies like *A Fish Called Wanda* and *De-Lovely*; Patti LuPone, who went on to star on Broadway in *Evita* and *Sweeney Todd*; and David Ogden Stiers, who played Major Charles Winchester on *M*A*S*H* for six years. In the class behind them were Robin Williams and Christopher Reeve. Imagine all that talent in one place at one time.

The story is that one day Houseman went into Margot's office and said, "We can't let these guys graduate and start doing toothpaste commercials. That would be a sin against mankind. We need to start a repertory company and allow them to hone their skills for a few years before they are ready for the big time."

And thus, The Acting Company was born. It still exists today in largely the same form as it did in 1972. The Company hires twelve to fifteen actors each year for a six-month gig. They rehearse two plays for a month—one of them is always a Shakespeare—and then they tour the country for four or five months. They try to appear in small towns across the country and bring live theater to places that have never been exposed to it.

This is a good thing that they have done and continue to do— and not just for the actors, but also for the communities to which they travel and perform. Judging from the letters that we used to receive from folks who had seen a show, they were often life changing. We frequently saw letters telling of how kids, who had never seen live theater until they saw an Acting Company performance, were now applying to drama schools following their high school graduation.

In addition to Kevin, Patti, and David, the company helped to develop a number of other stars: Jesse Martin from *Law & Order*, Frances Conroy from *Six Feet Under*, and Harriet Harris from *Desperate Housewives* come to mind. The company produced real acting pros. One time I heard Patti LuPone say that on that very day, 85 percent of all alumni of The Acting Company were gainfully employed in the theater.

One of the side benefits of being involved with The Acting Company was the chance to meet some pretty famous people. Over the years, Bonita and I were fortunate to have met and spoken, often at length, with not only Kevin and Patti, but also Angela Lansbury, Edgar Lansbury, Carol Burnett, Mike Farrell, Shelly Fabares, Robin Williams, Kathleen Turner, and Burt Reynolds. These were great times. And they produced great memories.

The hard part of the job was chairing the Finance Committee. As I recall, the company's operating budget was well over $2 million per year. And 80 percent of this money was funded by individual donations. Raising these funds every year was hard work for smart boys and girls.

Our biggest fund-raiser each year was the annual Masquerade Gala, held on the last Monday evening of October. We would usually attract 250 to 300 people and raise in excess of $500,000. It was a black-tie affair, and it was always held at some swanky Manhattan location like Cipriani. It was the epitome of class and elegance, with a little theatrical whimsy thrown in for good measure. The gala was my first exposure to The Acting Company, and Bonita and I attended for maybe four years before I joined the board.

Each year, the Company honored someone with the John Houseman Award for their "profound commitment to developing American actors and building a diverse audience for the theater." Among the recipients of the award were Harold Prince, Tony Randall, Jack O'Brien, Angela Lansbury, and Marian Seldes.

At the 1998 gala, The Acting Company presented the John Houseman Award to Burt Reynolds for his lifelong work in young people's theater. Bonita and I had decided to take our oldest daughter, Katie, and allow her to invite her close friend Jessie to the gala. Both girls had a real interest in theater and were very active in the Drama Department at Greenwich High School.

Our limo dropped us at the Copacabana at seven o'clock. We made our way to the bar, ordered drinks and sodas, and checked out the digs. The Copa was a famous New York landmark. It opened in 1940 and hit its peak in popularity in the 1950s and 1960s. By the late 1980s, the Copacabana had become a very cool nightclub with a lot of rich history.

A few minutes later, I spotted Burt Reynolds and pointed him out to the ladies. They were all aflutter and wanted to meet him but were scared to approach him. I led all three of them up to Burt, who was standing by himself at the other end of the bar.

"Hi, Burt. I'm Kurt Krauss," I said as we shook hands.

"Hi, Kurt," he responded. "I'm Burt Reynolds. It's nice to meet you."

"Burt," I continued, "I'd like to introduce my wife, Bonita; my daughter, Katie; and her best friend, Jesse. They are all big fans, but they were a little skittish about meeting you."

"Well hello, ladies," Burt said, turning on the charm. "It is my pleasure to meet you. There's nothing to be nervous about; I'm just a normal guy."

"So, Burt," I asked, "what do you think of the Copacabana?"

"This is my first time here," he answered. "It's a pretty cool place. I feel like I've stepped back into the 1950s."

About that time, I saw a buddy of mine across the room. So I left the three ladies taking with Burt, and I went to catch up with my friend. I sort of lost track of time, and it was about twenty minutes later when I looked around to see my wife engaged in an animated conversation with Mr. Reynolds. Just then, my daughter came rushing up to me.

"Dad … Dad! Burt is trying to pick up Mom. You've got to do something!" she blurted out.

"Oh, don't worry, Katie," I said. "Your mom will be fine. She's a big girl."

When I finally caught up with Bonita, she said that she and Burt had gotten into a conversation about Florida. He told her that he lived at Hobe Sound on the east coast. She told him that we had a place in Naples. He suggested that we both come over and visit him sometime and gave her his phone number.

Katie had heard bits and pieces of this conversation and was sure that Burt was on the make and was going after Mom. Even after she heard the whole story, Katie kept a close eye on Burt for the rest of the evening.

At every Masquerade, the company hired six or eight transvestites to mingle with the crowd and spice things up. These guys were unbelievable. They were usually dressed in long, tight-fitting, sequined gowns. They wore lots of boas and feathers and jewelry, and very high heels. Some of them were drop-dead gorgeous. They were a sight to behold.

One year, when Bonita was in the ladies' room, one of the transvestites had walked in. Bonita said to him, "You use the ladies' room?"

"What do you think?" he answered. "Would you suggest that I walk into the men's room dressed like this?"

"I guess not," Bonita replied as she made a hasty exit from the ladies' room.

At one gala, we were sitting with friends at our table just after finishing dinner, when up walked one of the transvestite regulars. We knew him from several earlier galas.

He walked up to me and asked, "Do you wanna dance?"

"Sure," I said, finishing my fifth scotch of the evening.

He took my arm, and I led us to the dance floor. We made it to the center and turned to face one another. I imagine we made quite a spectacle.

"I'll lead," he said to me.

"Like hell you will," I replied.

"Okay, big boy. Give it your best shot," he countered as he turned and fell back into my arms.

Now this was no small person. I'd estimate that he was six-foot-two and weighed two hundred pounds. I was barely able to catch him. But then we started dancing. It was a fast dance, and we were taking up more and more of the dance floor, what with all the spins and twists and do-si-dos.

One by one, the other dancers left the dance floor to make room for us. Finally, it was only Patti LuPone and her partner on the floor with us. At that point, my partner and I executed a world-class thunder clap followed by a double reverse turn, and we damned near crashed straight into Patti. The audience held their breath.

At the time, Patti was starring on Broadway in *Noises Off*, and I could just imagine the headlines in the New York papers the next morning:

Broadway Star Crushed in a Transvestite Dancing Incident

We continued to dance and executed some pretty nifty moves, if I do say so myself. Patti eventually sat down— perhaps because she was getting tired … or perhaps because she was beginning to fear for her safety.

When the dance was over, I walked back to my seat to limited applause and considerable catcalling. I found Bonita hiding under our table. My good friend Don Cogman had also taken a seat at our table.

"That was great," Don said somewhat facetiously.

"Yeah," I said. "I wonder why he picked me."

"That's easy," Don replied. "I paid him $20.00."

More Crazy Days

Follow the words of Lazarus Long: Sure the game is rigged.
But don't let that stop you; if you don't bet you can't win.

Hot Stuff

I love hot food: buffalo wings, Szechuan Chinese, Sri Lankan dishes, all of it. I like it when the tears run down my cheeks. I like it when the sweat breaks out on my brow. I like it when my lips seem to be on fire. I love hot food.

This all started maybe forty years ago. I started putting a little hot sauce on my tacos and a little horseradish on by beef. Then I started escalating to hotter sauces and more of them. The science works something like this:

> The hot, spicy taste of foods is not, in fact, a taste sensation but a feeling of pain. Capsaicin – the chemical compound that makes chili peppers hot – binds to proteins, or pain receptors, of nerve cells in the mucous membranes of the nose and mouth. The nerve impulses produced in this way pass via the trigeminal nerve into the brain, creating a painful burning feeling. The same receptors also react to heat, so that when heavily spiced food is eaten hot, the effect is even more intense. However, the pain is offset by the body's reaction, which is to release endorphins – naturally occurring opioids that produce a feeling of well-being – which could explain the popularity of hot, spicy food. (From "8

Ways to Naturally Increase Endorphins," Reader's
Digest Editors, RD.com)

This feeling of well-being is what drug users call a "high." And
in order to recreate it, a person needs to consume more and more
of the substance or activity that is causing the endorphin release.
Intense physical activity like running will cause this; so will drugs
like cocaine.

My "drug" of choice is hot food—really hot food. I actually
like the flavor of hot and spicy food. And while the pain can be
uncomfortable, the endorphin rushes more than make up for it.

My major hot wing phase began in the early 1980s in Atlanta.
The entire family's eatery of choice was a great little bar named the
Rusty Nail. It had ten wooden booths, a U-shaped bar that seated
maybe twenty, sawdust on the floors, an oldies jukebox, pinball
machines, darts, very cold beer, and bar food that included the best
chicken wings in town. And when you asked for them hot, they
made them hot. Cry your eyes out hot.

As I said, the entire family loved the Rusty Nail. We frequently
went there as a family, often for Sunday brunch after church. And
Bonita and I would spend an evening there at least once a month. We
would stop in after an Atlanta Hawks basketball game, or we would
spend an evening there watching a football game on TV.

I remember in 1991, I took my four-year-old son there one
Saturday for lunch. Joe was already a connoisseur of buffalo wings,
and he loved them hot. That day, our bartender was Susie, a very
attractive thirty-something blonde with a wonderfully outgoing
personality. Joe and I ordered up a plate of hot wings and beer for
me and soda for him.

As we were enjoying our wings, Joe began to ask me a series of
questions. I had no idea where he was headed.

"Dad," he asked, "when you and Mom go out at night by
yourselves, what is that called?"

"Well, Joe," I said, "it's called a date."

"Sometimes you come here on your dates, don't you, Dad?" he continued.

"Yes, son, sometimes we come here on dates," I answered.

"So do you ask Mom for a 'date' before you go out?" he asked.

"Well, yes, I guess I do," I responded.

He went back to eating his wings and drinking his soda.

About ten minutes later, Susie came over to check on us.

"Is everything okay," she queried.

"It's all great," I told her.

Then Joe, my charming little four-year-old son, looked up at her and asked, "Can I have a date?"

Susie was clearly flustered, but she recovered very quickly. "Joe," she said, "you come back here in twenty years, and I'll give you a date that you never will forget."

"Okay, that'll be great," Joe responded happily.

Joe is twenty-nine now. I sometimes wonder if he ever went back.

Several years earlier, we were getting ready for another New Year's Eve party. Several of our closest family and friends had ventured to Atlanta a day early so we could spend some quality time together before the masses descended.

That evening, the ladies decided to go to a movie, so the guys decided to go out for dinner. I had heard that the bowling alley in Greenwich was supposedly serving amazing buffalo wings. So off we went to the bowling alley. The group included my four closest lifetime friends: Gail Hamilton, Ron Comer, Jim Bachman, and my cousin Bill Krauss.

The place was called, appropriately enough, Greenwich Lanes. It doesn't seem to be in business today, but it was your standard bowling alley with maybe twenty lanes and a big bar off to the side.

We sat down and ordered some cold beers, and we talked to the bartender about the wings.

"I understand that you have the best hot wings in town," I said.

"That's what they tell me," he replied.

"Well just how hot are they?"

"The cook says he can make them as hot as you want."

"Well is the cook a real manly man?" I asked. "When he says 'hot,' is this a manly-man hot? Or a wimpy-guy hot?"

"I don't know," the bartender replied. "But no one has ever complained about them not being hot enough."

"Okay," I said. "I can't speak for the other guys, but I want twenty hot wings, and I want you to tell the chef that I very much doubt that he can make them hot enough for me."

The rest of the boys ordered up some mild, girlie-man wings, and we went back to drinking our beers. From this point forward, the story is best told by Cousin Bill, who had a better perspective than I to see exactly what happened. Here is what he reported:

> About twenty minutes later, the bartender came into the bar from the kitchen carrying several platters of hot wings. We knew that something was up as our eyes began to water when the waiter was still thirty feet away from us. The closer he got, the more our eyes burned.
>
> He set two platters of wings in front of us, and another in front of Kurt. So help me, you could see lethal vapors rising from his platter. Kurt readied himself, took a deep breath, and ate the first wing. "Umm," he said, and then he took another.
>
> After maybe three wings, tears were beginning to form in his eyes. The sweat was collecting on his brow. His face was turning red. Meanwhile, the rest of us were trying to eat our wings, but we were having trouble breathing because the steam and

vapors coming from Kurt's platter of wings were overpowering.

"How does he do it?" I thought to myself.

After about five wings, Kurt paused. The sweat was still forming on his brow and his eyes were still watering. And then a drop of sweat ran down his forehead and down his nose and dripped onto the table.

"Whew!" he said. And then he got off of his stool and proceeded to walk around the bar. I thought that he was going to the men's room. But it turned out that he was just trying to collect himself.

He completed his walk around the bar and sat back down. He looked at the bartender, who was standing there taking in this amazing spectacle, and said in a low voice, "Can I please have some Tabasco sauce?"

We all about died. The Tabasco sauce came, and he poured it on his remaining fifteen wings. He ate every last one. When he was done, he called for the bartender.

The bartender came over, and Kurt said, "One more Rolling Rock, please; and oh yeah, my compliments to the cook. With just a little extra Tabasco, the wings were perfect!"

What a man!

Without question, the best Hot Stuff story took place in Beaconsfield, England. A group of us were working with a client in London and were over there for the week. Gary Shows and I were from Atlanta. Adam Zauder was from Chicago. And my partner John Smith, who worked in our firm's London office, lived just outside the city in the small village of Penn.

John's family was out of town, so all of us were staying at his house. After we finished work at about eight o'clock, we jumped in his car and headed to Penn. Along the way, John suggested that we have Indian food for dinner. Both Gary and I were against the idea, but we didn't want to rain on John's parade. So we employed a more subtle strategy.

"Okay, John," Gary said. "But first, let's go to that pub near your house and have a pint or three."

"Do you mean the Old Queen's Head?" John asked.

"Yeah, that's the one," Gary said.

And off we went to the pub. Gary and I figured that if we drank for several hours, the Indian food restaurant would be closed and we could just eat a sandwich at John's house.

We didn't leave the Old Queen's Head until it closed at eleven. I was sure that we had avoided Indian food for the evening. As we got into the car, John said, "And now for some Indian food."

"John, it's after eleven," I said. "They have to be closed, don't they?"

"Oh no," John replied. "There is a great Indian restaurant in Beaconsfield that's open until four. We'll be there in five minutes."

All of us were pretty well-lubed when we got to the restaurant. As we went in the front door, I suggested to the manager that he seat us way in the back, away from as many customers as possible, because I felt a case of severe rowdiness coming on.

We ordered another round of beers and then talked with the waiter about our dinner orders. "Do you want curried this?" he asked. "Or curried that? Or we have curried the other."

We settled on something curried, but then I asked him to tell the chef to make my dish hot. "Very hot," I said. "In fact, as hot as he can possibly make it."

When our food arrived, I took a bite of my extra, extra hot curried something or other. It wasn't hot. Not even close. Any self-respecting wing joint would have likely called it medium. Or maybe even mild/medium.

Being half in the bag did not help me at this point. I called the waiter and asked him to go back to the chef and have him send me the hottest thing that he had in the kitchen.

The waiter returned a few minutes later with a little saucer that held four small, dark-green peppers, each about one inch long. He said that the chef had assured him that these were the hottest things in the kitchen. In fact, the chef had said that these might be the hottest things in metropolitan London.

"Try them at your own risk," the waiter said.

My later research suggested that these were bird's eye chilies. The hotness of peppers is measured by something called Scoville units. A bird's eye chili produces about 200,000 Scovilles. By comparison, a jalapeño pepper clocks in at about 5,000 Scovilles. This meant that the peppers we were about to eat were around forty times hotter than a jalapeño. Whew!

The moment of truth had arrived. John decided to let good sense prevail and took a pass on his pepper. But Gary, Adam, and I were brave; we'd also been drinking beer for four hours. We each took a little green pepper, popped it in our mouths, chewed it up, and swallowed it.

"That wasn't so bad," I said, just before the tsunami hit me.

All of a sudden, my mouth was on fire. My throat started to severely constrict, and I couldn't breathe. I couldn't talk. I couldn't scream. I was seriously wondering if I had accidently killed myself. My two pepper-poppin' padres were in similar distress.

We got up and sprinted to the men's room, where we all three crowded around the sink and splashed cold water on our faces. Slowly, we began to recover. Our throat constrictions began to relax, and we could take short breaths. We were finally able to speak. While still sweating profusely, we began to recover most of our bodily functions. We stayed in the restroom for maybe twenty minutes, after which time we were able to return to the table.

Conversation ensued about just how hot those hot peppers had been. None of us had every experienced anything like it. I ordered some more beers to try to get us cooled off, and we all began to get back to normal.

Then I had a great idea. It was probably brought on by the beer. But I have been known to come up with some pretty stupid ideas while stone-cold sober.

"No one," I said, "would ever eat more than one of those bad boys on purpose. It wouldn't happen. It couldn't happen. The near-death experience was just too real. But we have one pepper left. If we cut it into three pieces and each eat one third of it, we would most certainly set a world record."

"You're nuts," said Gary. "Don't you guys ever learn from experience?"

"I'm in," said Adam.

So we cut the last little green assassin in half, and Adam and I each popped, chewed, and swallowed another piece of bird's eye chili.

I fully expected another painful reaction, but I thought it would be only half as intense as the first one. Boy was I wrong. This one took up where the first one had left off. I couldn't breathe. I couldn't talk. It was back to the men's room for another twenty minutes of cold water therapy.

This had to be one of the dumbest stunts that I had ever pulled. My reactions to the bird's eye chilies had been very unpleasant and downright painful. They were also scary. And I was in so much discomfort that I don't remember any endorphin rush. Why, I asked myself later, did I decide that this was a good idea?

Adam and I took solace in the fact that we now undoubtedly held two world's records: one was for eating the most bird's eye chilies in history; the other was for being the two dumbest people on the planet.

Fall Foliage

B ack in 1987, my partners Jim Wolf and John "Rock" Rockwell and I sold an assignment to a company in Boston, Massachusetts. They were a very large, very old silversmith, who first began production in 1857. They also had a sizeable housewares division that sold everything from toasters to teakettles to flowerpots. Let's call them Knives & Forks Inc.

Their sales had fallen off over several years, and their CEO, Lennie France, retained us to help them figure out how to grow their sales and revenue. Jim, Rock, and I and our team had been at it for only about two weeks when Jim and I came to a major revelation. We were sitting in a conference room in Booz Allen's New York office at about seven thirty on a Friday night when both of us had a "Eureka!" moment at exactly the same time.

"These guys are running out of cash," Jim said.

"Yep," I answered. "I figure they will run out in six weeks."

We flew home for the weekend and were back in the New York office first thing Monday morning. Jim and I took our findings to Rock, and the three of us determined what to do and when to do it. We were sure that we would have to get rid of the senior management team and take the company into Chapter 11 bankruptcy. We then tried to identify potential pathways to get the company viable again using the protections that the bankruptcy laws provided. We strongly felt we could restructure the company into a viable enterprise in six to nine months; therefore, we decided to move forward on that plan.

The first step was to call a meeting with the CEO, COO, and CFO to review our findings and conclusions with them. Since Knives & Forks Inc. was a public company, it had a board of directors with several outside, independent directors. We decided it would be very helpful if one or two of those directors could attend the meeting as well, but we had to get them invited quietly so that the whole leadership team didn't run for cover and stonewall any action plan.

Rock was personal friends with one outside director, who was the CEO of a major company headquartered in Ohio. So he called him up and explained the situation.

"Can you find a reason to be in Boston next Tuesday?" Rock asked him. "We don't want to alarm Lennie, so find some nonthreatening reason to show up. And see if you can get another director to join you."

The director apparently told Lennie that he and another director were planning to be in Boston on Tuesday and that they were both free in the afternoon.

"That's great," said Lennie. "Booz Allen is delivering their first progress report Tuesday afternoon. Why don't you guys sit in?"

Mission accomplished.

On Tuesday afternoon, the progress meeting took place. In attendance were Lennie and his COO and CFO; the two outside directors; and Rock, Jim, me, and three Booz Allen staff members. Rock led off the meeting.

"Gentlemen, about three weeks ago we began an assignment to determine how to achieve higher sales and margins for Knives & Forks Inc. In the course of our analysis, we came to a rather startling conclusion. The company is basically broke. We estimate that it will run out of cash early next month and that Chapter 11 bankruptcy is the only viable option for dealing with the situation."

Rock continued, "Now, we also think that we have determined the reasons behind this calamitous situation. The CEO can't lead. The COO can't manage. And the CFO doesn't know the numbers."

Rock then wrapped up his stirring introduction by saying, "Kurt will now fill you in on the details."

Thanks a lot, Rock. Just hand me a steaming pile of crap, why don't you.

I made the presentation. The outside directors took over the process and said we would report to them from now on. And they endorsed our plan for moving things forward.

Four weeks later, Lennie, the CFO, and the COO were gone, the company had filed for bankruptcy protection, and two Booz Allen principals were running the company as acting CEO and acting CFO.

Six months later, Knives & Forks Inc. emerged from bankruptcy with all of its core businesses and 75 percent of its original employees still in place. It was a demanding and challenging assignment. But we were able to get them through this difficult time and come out the other side stronger than ever. We also had a lot of fun in Boston.

We must have started to work for Knives & Forks Inc. in August, because we had been there about two months when I decided that it would be a good idea to organize a fall foliage tour for mid-October. New England has perhaps the best, most vibrant fall foliage colors in the country. And we were working in Boston, the gateway to New England.

I was able to get five couples to sign up for the three-day weekend trip. Three Booz Allen members of the Knife & Fork Inc. team, in addition to Bonita and me, joined in the fun: Bob Morin and his girlfriend, Babs; Gary Shows and his significant other, Susan; and Jason Schmidt and his date, Chloe. My roommate from graduate school, Jim Bachman, and his girlfriend, Margie, also agreed to come along.

We decided that an RV was the best way for ten people to travel through New England for three days. We thought better of trying to sleep everyone in the RV and instead booked hotels. In retrospect, staying on the bus might have been interesting.

The fun began late Friday afternoon. Bob, Gary, Jason, and I left the client at about four thirty and went to rent a Winnebago. We got a nice thirty-eight-foot RV and headed to the liquor store. After stocking up with more than enough cold beer, wine, and liquor, we headed for Logan Airport.

We had told the six folks who were flying into Boston that we would be illegally parked, directly across the street from the main entrance to Terminal C, and to make their way there and look for a big Winnebago. We got to the airport at about six o'clock, parked as planned, and opened the bar. People started drifting in about six thirty and joined in the party. Bob Morin was the last to arrive at about a quarter to eight, and since he was sober, he was elected to drive.

We took the RV into downtown Boston to a landmark old restaurant named Locke-Ober's. It was located at 3 Winter Street, which was little more than a dead-end alley. The Winnebago damned near took up the whole street. I told Bob to "park it," and we all went into the restaurant. I found out later that Bob gave the valet parking attendant $20, and he took it from there. After a gourmet meal, some after-dinner drinks, and a little fruit and cheese, we got up to leave. Our RV was parked right outside the door. We loaded up and went to the Hyatt in Cambridge for the first night of our weekend adventure.

We were all up bright and early the next morning, ready to get things underway. Over breakfast we agreed to some ground rules: first, each of the guys would drive for two hours each day; second, no alcohol until after your driving shift was done for the day; and third, we would drive from 8:00 a.m. until 6:00 p.m. each day.

We headed out of Boston and worked our way up through Massachusetts and into Vermont. The foliage was unbelievable: bright oranges, vibrant yellows, breathtaking reds. None of us had seen a display quite like this. And the farther north we drove, the prettier it got.

We traveled almost all the way up through Vermont and then started coming back south through New Hampshire. Our final destination of the day was Whitefield, New Hampshire, at the north end of the White Mountains, near Mount Washington, the most prominent mountain east of the Mississippi River. It was right around six o'clock when we pulled into our accommodations for the night.

The Spalding Inn Club was built in the nineteenth century and was initially known as the Cherry Hill House. It was a classic, old New England inn. Its main claim to fame was its lawn bowling court: 120' x 19' of perfectly manicured bent grass. The American Lawn Bowling Association often held their National Championship at the Spalding Inn Club.

This quaint New England Inn was the perfect ending for a wonderful day. We assembled at eight o'clock for drinks and dinner. Remember that some of us had already been drinking for most of the day; we went into the evening feeling no pain.

During dinner, Bob Morin—who had consumed his share of alcohol during the day—tapped his water glass with his spoon to get everyone's attention. "Folks," Bob started, "I will bet any or all of you $100 each that later tonight, after everyone is asleep, I can get the Winnebago into the middle of the lawn bowling court without damaging one blade of grass."

The group was aflutter. Most thought that it would be impossible. There was absolutely no way to get the RV onto the court without tearing up the grounds. Others tried to figure out how. Could he use planks to spread the weight? Could he use a crane to suspend, move, and drop the Winnebago? Where in the hell would he get a crane at three o'clock on Sunday morning? But if this made no sense, why was Bob willing to make nine $100 bets?

There were multiple conversations going on in loud voices, and most of the other dinners were starting to get really pissed. The one person who was not pissed was the general manager of the Spalding Inn Club, Stuart Winthrop. Stu was scared to death. Our rowdy band of revelers was threatening to destroy his beloved lawn bowling court. He could only imagine the mud and the ruts and the damage that our Winnebago would cause.

He came over to our table to talk with us. It was very clear that he was not angry; he was truly frightened. "I heard you guys talking about moving your RV to the lawn bowling court. I don't think that is very funny. You shouldn't kid about something like that."

"I wasn't kidding, Stu," Bob responded. "I really think I can get it on there without damaging one blade of grass."

"You can't be serious. You will destroy it. And we're having a regional tournament here next weekend."

"Do you want to get in on the bet, Stu?" Bob asked.

"No!" Stu yelled. "I want you guys to quit thinking about the lawn bowling court; it is officially off-limits to you. Don't make me call the police."

"Jeez, Stu," Bob said. "Chill out! So if I promise not to try to put the Winnebago onto the lawn bowling court, what's in it for us?"

"How about free drinks all around?" Stu offered, finally believing that there might be a way out of this.

"Nah, we've all had enough to drink today. We want more of an outdoor activity."

"What sort of outdoor activity?"

"Well, I noticed that you have an outdoor pool. Maybe we could go for a midnight swim," Bob suggested.

"I'm sorry, but the pool is closed for the season."

"Well, does it still have water in it?"

"Yes. We just closed it yesterday, and we aren't going to drain it until next week."

"If there is water it in, why can't we go for a swim?"

"I think that the owners would get upset if I were to let you do that," Stu declared.

"No problem," said Bob. "Who wants in on the Winnebago bet?"

"Hold on," said Stu, with desperation in his voice. "If I let you go for a midnight swim, do you promise that no harm will come to the lawn bowling court?"

"You have my word," Bob promised.

"Deal!" said Stu as he walked off to get the pool gate keys.

"What the hell was that all about, Bob?" Gary asked.

"Well, I thought that a midnight swim sounded fun. I saw the sign said 'Closed for Season,' but I also saw that there was water in the pool. I knew I had to come up with something really big to get Stu to let us swim. I figured if he was faced with something that could damage his precious lawn bowling court, he would fold like a cheap suitcase." Bob and Babs had their midnight swim—sans suits, I would guess.

The next day, we traveled through Vermont and New Hampshire and stopped by John and Lorraine Rockwell's home in Kennebunkport, Maine. Needless to say, we were in no shape to be making house calls.

We got back to Boston Sunday evening. On Monday morning, Jim and the ladies flew home. The rest of us went back to work.

What foliage. What a trip. What memories.

Streaks

I love to play blackjack. And I have a system that has proven to be a winner over many years. I don't count cards. I don't play negative progressions. I don't play Oscar's system. I play what is known as a modified positive progression system. I call it "streaks."

Merriam-Webster's defines a "streak" as:

A period of repeated success or failure, e.g.:
- A lucky streak
- A winning or losing streak
- A hot streak

The basis of this strategy is that streaks exist. We see this everywhere. Baseball players have hitting streaks, usually followed by batting slumps. Did the ball suddenly get smaller? Did the pitchers suddenly get better? Did the player's eyesight suddenly improve? No. They were just experiencing streaks.

Did you ever have a day where everything seems to go your way? You make every light on the way to work. Then your boss gives you a raise. Then you finish a big project on time and under budget. It is one of those days where, as they say, "Everything you touch turns to gold." Well, I contend that you are just on a hot streak.

After thirty-plus years of playing high-stakes blackjack, I find that the same sort of streaks occur with great frequency in games of chance. When they start to develop, you begin to play them. As they extend, you play them stronger. When they stop, you stop. It's as simple as that.

Under the typical rules of blackjack, the house has about a 4.5 percent advantage over the player, virtually all a result of the rule that says once a player busts (i.e., goes over twenty-one), they lose their bet, even if the dealer eventually busts as well. But 4.5 percent is not a big number. Statistically speaking, it means that out of 1000 hands of blackjack, the dealer should win 522 hands and the player should win 478. But that is before the impact of streaks.

Here is how streaks pay off for me at the blackjack table. Most of the time there is a steady back and forth of winning and losing hands between me and the dealer. The house will win a few hands. Then I will do likewise. I'd say that this win-a-few, lose-a-few situation is going on 90 percent of the time that I'm at the table. Neither I nor the house is making a major dent in the bankroll of the other. During these periods, I make my standard bet of $25 or £25 per hand.

At some point, I notice the early stages of a possible streak. I win one hand, then two, then three. And I am winning with magical draws. I hit a fourteen and get a seven. The dealer reveals two face cards for twenty. I am not yet on a streak, but the signs are promising.

At that point, I simply double my bet and see what develops. If I win a couple of more hands, I double my bet again. And I try to look for ways to get more money into the game by splitting pairs or doubling down. Doubling down is a bet permitted in most casinos whereby if the player's card count is a total of nine, ten, or eleven on the deal, they can double their bet and receive one card. They are hoping for a face card, which gives them a strong hand if the dealer's up card is anything shaky.

Splitting is an option allowed by all casinos. If the player receives any natural pair on the deal, they may double their bet and split their cards into two hands, receiving an additional card on each. This is pretty cool if you have a pair of eights, giving you a horrible card count of sixteen, and if the dealer is showing a five, suggesting that they are very likely to bust. When it works like it should, the player ends up with two high-count hands, the dealer busts, and the player wins double the amount of their initial bet.

One of the dumbest plays in blackjack is to split a natural pair of tens. Your almost-sure winner of twenty will often turn into a fourteen and a seventeen, two likely losers. But when I'm on a killer streak, I've been known to do just that. I want to get more money in play, and I have this surreal confidence that the dealer is going to lose. Remember, the dealer is on a cold streak at the same time that you are tearing it up.

And then I may start playing two hands/boxes on each deal. And then I might double my bet again. I keep doing this until I lose two hands in a row. At that point, I back off of my aggressive betting and play for less. When I lose the third hand, I declare victory and go back to $25 a hand. From a $25 starting point, I've had as much as $500 on the table on just one deal. And I've had streaks last for twenty or more hands.

I don't win every time I play blackjack. I always make my standard bet $25 or £25 per hand, and I always sit down with a $1000 or a £1000 stake in my pocket. When my stake is gone, I'm done for the night. But I win about 70 percent of the time. Over a four-year period, I kept precise records of my winnings and loses while gambling at the Ritz Club in London. I played on perhaps thirty occasions, and my accumulative winnings were $17,800. That is why I play streaks.

One time back in the late 1990s, I was in London on business. One of my senior finance staff, Tom Phillips, was spending six months in London to address a number of financial issues. We spent many evenings together when I was visiting. Tom loved to play blackjack too, and we often ended up at the Ritz Club.

One night we sat down at a table and began to play. Forty minutes went by, and we had only seen the steady back and forth of winning and losing against the dealer. Then I saw a streak begin to materialize. I began to increase my bet and get more aggressive in my play. Tom continued to make his standard wager of £10 per hand.

I won maybe £150 on that first streak. Then I caught a second streak and then a third. Tom meanwhile was plodding along at £10 per hand and winning and losing at about the same rate. He experienced the same three streaks as I did—since during a streak the dealer busts a disproportionate amount of the time—but he never cashed in on it. It was £10 bet after £10 bet.

At the Ritz Club, you are not allowed to drink alcoholic beverages at the gaming tables. Apparently, this was the British government's attempt to keep you from getting all liquored up and losing the rent money. Anyway, after maybe two hours of gambling, Tom and I moved to the bar for a little refreshment.

As we were sitting at the bar nursing our drinks, I brought up the notion of streaks. "Look, Tom," I said. "Didn't you see what just happened back there? You made your standard £10 bet on every hand. Are you winning?"

"No," Tom replied. "I'm down £30. But I'll get it back."

I decided that a lecture was in order. I gave Tom my whole spiel about streaks and ended by saying in a loud voice, "I've played three streaks tonight, and I'm up £450."

Tom proceeded to loudly inform me that I couldn't tell my ass from third base. "You should know better," he said. "You were a math major in college, weren't you? Every hand is an independent event. If you're not counting cards, then your probability of winning is the same on every hand. And your £450 in winnings was just luck, pure and simple."

At about this time, I noticed a distinguished looking gentleman leaving his seat at the other end of the bar and walking in our direction. He came up between us and said directly to Tom, "Sir, if you don't believe in streaks, you should never sit down at a blackjack table again."

Tom, in a somewhat arrogant tone of voice, said, "And who might you be?"

"I am Samuel Benedict, and I am the chairman of the Department of Mathematics at Princeton University. Good evening, gentlemen."

And he turned and walked out of the bar. My hero!

First Class

T he travel demands on most management consultants are pretty much constant. Airplanes become your home away from home. Early in my career, I would typically leave home early on Monday morning, fly to some distant city, work all week, and fly home late on Friday. That's maybe one hundred flights per year.

Later in my career, I usually had at least two assignments underway at any given time, and of course they were often in different cities, if not different countries. Plus I held various firm leadership positions that required me to travel to yet other glamor spots, such as Cleveland, Ohio; Bethesda, Maryland; and Newark, New Jersey. During those years, I took on average maybe five flights a week. That's more than two hundred per year.

All in, over a twenty-nine-year career, I estimate that combining both business and pleasure trips, I took about five thousand flights. The hardest part was the majority of these flights took off either before 7:00 a.m. or after 7:00 p.m. We usually traveled on our own time.

Most veteran fliers develop a skill that allows them to cope with the frustration and uncertainty of flying. Canceled flights, screaming babies, long lines, delayed flights, rude gate agents, lost reservations, obnoxious passengers, and those yippy little dogs in their pet carriers can all combine to make you nuts. I found the only way to maintain your sanity was to learn how to go into the "airport trance." You literally close your eyes and then slowly reopen them in a semicatatonic state. You walk and talk and stand in line and obey stupid rules and tolerate bad behavior by using your self-induced stupor to transport you to calm, relaxing places, like the seashore or the forest or a nudist colony. This really works. The time speeds by, and the frustrations are muted.

During my twenty-nine-year business career, I was a partner at Booz Allen Hamilton; I owned my own firm, the Mead Point Group; and I was the chief financial officer at Burson-Marsteller, a large PR firm and the largest subsidiary of ad agency giant Young & Rubicam. At each one of these firms, the travel policy was that senior folks could fly first class. While this sounds like a nice perk, for big guys like me who flew all the time, it was more about survival.

I had any number of crazy days in the first-class cabin of an airliner. One time I was flying from New York to Singapore on Singapore Airlines, which at the time was rated the best carrier in the world. The quality of their first-class food, drink, and service was simply the best. Before we took off, the flight attendant came through the cabin taking drink orders to be served as soon as we were airborne.

"My name is Kim. May I bring you a drink after takeoff, Mr. Krauss?" the flight attendant asked.

"Yes," I said. "I'll have a Johnnie Walker Black Label on the rocks with a splash of water."

"Sir," he responded, "we don't serve Black Label. We only offer Blue Label. Will that be alright?"

It had been a long day, and I react a little strongly. "You mean to tell me that I pay all of this money to fly first class and you don't even carry Black Label. I've never heard of Johnnie Walker Blue Label. Is it a step down from Red Label? God help us. Go ahead and bring the cheap stuff, and I'll make do."

"Very well, sir," Kim said in a very respectful tone of voice.

A few minutes after takeoff, he returned with my drink: a Blue Label on the rocks with a splash of water. I thanked him, and he went on his way.

A short time later, I took a sip. Wow! This was probably the best blended scotch I had ever tasted. I rang my call button to summons Kim.

"Yes, Mr. Krauss," he said as he walked up to me. "How can I help you?"

"Kim, I might have been a little hasty in attacking Johnnie Walker Blue Label and in questioning why Singapore Air served it. This is clearly an extraordinary scotch. I've drunk Johnnie Walker for many years, but I've never heard of it. What is the story?"

"Last year Johnnie Walker came out with a new premium scotch—Blue Label. They claim that only one in ten thousand cases that they produce has the quality, character, and taste to make the grade as a Blue Label. Right now, they are not marketing it in the United States. It's only available in Asia, which explains why you've never heard of it. But you can find it in a duty-free shop over here. It sells for about $200 per bottle."

"Thanks, Kim," I said. "Sorry I lost my cool earlier. I should have known that Singapore Airlines would not be serving cheap scotch in first class. Sometimes I just open my mouth and insert my foot."

Another time I was flying from Newark to Detroit on an evening flight. Newark and the whole New York metropolitan area were in the midst of a blizzard, so flight delays and cancellations were common. Eventually our flight boarded, and it looked like we were going to go.

We taxied out toward the end of the runway, but stopped short of it. The pilot then announced that we had been put on a ground hold and would likely be sitting there for up to two hours before we took off. He said that the flight attendants would be serving drinks while we waited.

I knew that if I started drinking then, I would be sloshed by the time I got to Detroit. Plus I had some work to do, and I needed to be sober to do it. So I decided to delay my much-needed Johnnie Walker scotch until we took off.

I dove into the work and limited myself to water during our two-hour delay. But I was dreaming about my post-takeoff drink the whole time. At long last, the pilot announced that we were going to finally take off. I remember that there was snow covering the runway as we zoomed down it. And I also remember that the pilot said later that we were the last flight to make it out of Newark before they closed the airport.

As soon as the seat belt sign was turned off, the flight attendant came through the first-class cabin. "I'll finally have that drink now," I said. "Make it a double Johnnie Walker Black on the rocks with a splash of water, please."

"I'm sorry, sir," the flight attendant said, "but we've run out of ice."

So much for working hard, maintaining self-control, and postponing gratification; the old adage is true: no good deed goes unpunished!

⚫━━━⚫━━━⚫

Over the years, I met a number of celebrities who were also flying in first class. Not to name-drop, but at one time or another I flew with Lou Rawls, Faye Dunaway, Vanna White, Keith Richards, Bryant Gumbel, Dusty Baker, Garrison Keillor, and Sarah, the Duchess of York.

Traveling with Lou Rawls was a treat. We shared a five-hour flight from Atlanta to Los Angeles, and we talked all the way. I learned about his life and his career. He was equally curious about me and my career. Lou was one of the most sincerely nice people that I have ever met.

For you youngsters who are not familiar with Lou Rawls, he was a jazz, soul, and R&B singer who had a fifty-year career in the music business. He recorded some fifty-six albums and won three Grammy Awards during his career. Frank Sinatra once said that Rawls had "the classiest singing and silkiest chops in the singing game." He was a class act.

As the managing partner of Booz Allen's Atlanta office, I was the host of an annual formal dinner dance. I had brought in the Drifters as our dance band and entertainment the year before. And as I was talking with Lou Rawls, I had a great idea.

"Lou," I said, "we have a formal party every year for the partners and staff of the office. It's a group of maybe eighty people. And we always have entertainment. Why don't we hire you for our party next spring?"

"That would be great," Lou said. "It sounds like a lot more fun than most of my concerts."

"Instead of being the 'hired help,' you could be our invited guest. You could dine with us and party with us and get to know everybody. They are all good people," I offered. "But of course, we'd still compensate you," I added.

"How much were you thinking?" Lou asked.

"Well, we paid the Drifters $5,000 last year," I answered. "But I could go to $10,000 for the great Lou Rawls."

"Oh, no," Lou responded. "I couldn't do it for any less than $25,000. My manager would kill me."

"Hold on, Lou," I tried to counter. "You could come as my guest to a terrific party. You could bring a friend. You could dine on gourmet food. And after dinner, you could go to the stage and sing for maybe a half hour or forty minutes. Then you could rejoin the party. And we'd pay for your travel expenses and pay you ten grand. Why isn't that a good deal?"

"That is an extremely generous deal, Kurt," Lou replied. "If it were just me, I'd do it in a minute. But my manager oversees my business interests, and if I did this he would be furious. I just can't do it."

"Well, damn," I replied, and we moved on to talk about other things. I've often dreamed about how cool it would have been to have had Lou Rawls singing in a small room of eighty people. It would have been a night to remember.

•••━━━●━━━●••

My greatest first-class experience happened in 1981. The Major League Baseball All-Star Game was played in Cleveland that year, and we were living in Cleveland at that time. The game was played on Sunday night, August 9, and I watched it from my living room.

As I was watching the game, I noticed that the Los Angeles Dodgers had six players on the National League team. And then I remembered that I had a 7:00 a.m. flight from Cleveland to Los Angeles on Monday morning. I wondered if the Dodgers had a home stand coming up after the All-Star game. I found the Sunday paper and checked the Sports Section. Sure enough, the Dodgers had a 5:40 p.m. game in Los Angeles the next night, August 10. And even better, they were playing the Cincinnati Reds, who had three All-Stars on the NL team.

I reasoned that all nine of these guys would likely be on the first flight from Cleveland to Los Angeles the next morning and that they would all be traveling first class. I called my driver and told him to pick me up at 5:00 a.m. I wanted to get to the airport and get checked very early. I didn't want to get bumped.

I arrived at the airport long before most of the passengers on the Los Angeles flight. I got checked in and settled down with a cup of coffee and the morning paper. About a half hour before departure, here came the boys of summer. Sure enough, all nine ball players were taking the flight:

Fernando Valenzuela   Dave Conceptión
Davey Lopes   George Foster
Burt Hooton   Tom Seaver
Steve Garvey   Dusty Baker
Pedro Guerrero

After we boarded, I learned that all the first-class passengers were major leaguers except for me, one other lucky guy, and Bryant Gumbel, who had broadcast the game on national TV on Sunday night.

I was seated next to Dusty Baker. Tom Seaver and Steve Garvey were in the row ahead of me. Fernando Valenzuela, Davey Lopes, and George Foster were across the aisle. As a lifelong baseball fan, I was in heaven.

I had an interesting conversation about free agency with Dusty. His contract with the Dodgers was ending after the current season, and he was trying to figure out what to do: remain with Los Angeles or explore free agency. He was a pretty astute guy and laid out his options pretty clearly. We discussed them for over an hour. And of course, I had an opinion on each of them.

About midway through the flight, Tom Seaver stood up in the aisle and addressed the group.

"Did I ever tell you guys about my appearance on ABC's *The American Sportsman?*" he began. "Curt Gowdy and I went pheasant hunting in North Dakota. They set it up with us walking down this dirt trail, and as we neared a bunch of scrub bushes, they hoped that the pheasants that they had 'planted' in advance would take off and Curt and I could shoot them out of the sky. Unfortunately," he continued, "every time we got within two hundred feet of the pheasants, they would hear us and take off. But they were too far away for us to take a shot. We tried it about five times, each with the same result. Then someone from the show had the clever idea of mildly sedating the birds so that they would not startle as easily," Tom explained.

"When they had done the deed and placed the pheasants back in the scrub brush, Curt and I took our places up the trail. We slowly walked down the path, talking about this and that. Of course, they were filming and recording the entire time."

By this time, Seaver was walking up and down the first-class aisle and acting out the story. "We kept getting closer and closer to the birds, but they weren't moving," he said.

"Finally we got all the way up to the scrub brush, but still nothing was moving. I stuck out my left foot and kicked the bushes, and sure enough, the pheasants took off. Curt and I immediately hoisted our shotguns to our shoulders and blasted away."

Tom then said, "Have any of you guys seen what a pheasant looks like when it's been shot at point-blank range? It's basically just a handful of feathers, and a small handful at that. Needless to say, that footage never made it onto TV. The animal rights crowd would have had a fit."

What a story. What a time. What a flight.

Wigs

I like to play poker and roulette and craps—but I love to play blackjack. I've played at a number of casinos in Las Vegas, Reno, and Atlanta City, and at Foxwoods and the Mohegan Sun in Connecticut, but I'm not fond of US casinos. For me, they are too garish and too overdone. And their clientele is often troubling, too many overweight people in tank tops who look like they are losing the rent money. I don't mean to be judgmental. It's just not my cup of tea.

London, on the other hand, is a different story. There are over twenty casinos in metropolitan London, and many of them would remind you of their US counterparts. But there is also a small group of upscale casinos that are unlike anything I've seen in the United States. Most are located in Mayfair, perhaps the toniest area of London. There you'll find Les Ambassadeurs, where membership reportedly costs £25,000 per year; Aspinalls, of whom one reviewer said, "If James Bond were looking for a casino in Mayfair, he would probably end up at Aspinalls"; the Playboy Club, where I used to belong until it closed in the mid-1980s (it reopened in 2011, and membership is now very expensive and very selective); and Crockfords Casino, the oldest private gaming club in London, established in 1828.

But my favorite casino is, without question, the Ritz Club, located in the lower level of the Ritz Hotel on Piccadilly Street. It has always been an elegant and classy establishment with a terrific clientele. Rich people, yes, but without the arrogance and sense of entitlement that often accompanies such folks. The restaurant is world-class, and the bar is small and intimate. Most of all, it's the people. Over the years, I got to know many of the bartenders, waiters, dealers, pit bosses, managers, and service staff. They were, with only one exception, terrific people. I won't go into detail about the exception aside from saying that he was the casino manager and he was a total jerk.

During my career, I visited London many, many times. I would say that I made at least one hundred trips to London between 1980 and 2000. And I always stayed at my home away from home: the Ritz Hotel. There, too, I knew many of the staff, and they would always go out of their way to help me and to make me feel welcome.

I would usually visit the Ritz Club at least once during each trip. Sometimes I'd visit by myself for only a couple of hours; other times I would take a client for drinks, dinner, and gambling, and we would be there for the entire evening. I have entertained family, friends, clients, and staff at the Ritz Club over the years. No one has ever been disappointed.

So imagine my shock when I learned that the Ritz Club was closing. Here is the story: The casino was owned by the Ritz Hotel, but they subcontracted the management and operation of the casino to a group called London Clubs International. This arrangement had been going on for many years. In 1997, the agreement between the Ritz and LCI was up for renewal. There were rumored problems in the negotiation, but everyone was confident that an agreement would be reached. That is until LCI announced that they weren't renewing the agreement and instead were opening their own casino two blocks away. The name of the new casino and its address were the same: 50 St James.

A pall fell over the Ritz Club and its staff and members. "No Ritz Club?" people lamented. "It can't be true." But sure enough, the doors were closed on June 30, 1997, and that was that ... or so we thought.

I was sitting in my office in Greenwich, Connecticut, later that summer when I received a letter. It was from a gentleman named Mike Steele who claimed to represent the interests of the two relatively new owners of the Ritz Hotel: Sir William and Sir Edward Clay, two of the richest men in England. It seemed that they had decided they should reopen the Ritz Club and operate it themselves. But in order to do that, they would need to get approval and a license from the Gaming Board of Great Britain, as the club had been operating under the license of LCI while they had been running the show.

No one thought that this would present a problem, but Mr. Steele was trying to cover all his bases. He asked if I would be willing to write a letter supporting the Ritz Club's license application.

"We are asking some long-standing members to voice their support to the Gaming Board. We're not really concerned; we just to make sure that we have no issues."

I wrote a very supportive and encouraging letter and sent it off.

I hadn't heard anything for a couple of months, when one day I got a phone call from Mike Steele. "I wanted to thank you for your gracious letter of support to the Gaming Board," he said. "But unfortunately it wasn't enough; they denied our application, claiming there were already enough upscale casinos in London and there was no need for another."

"You've got to be kidding," I replied. "This sounds like economic planning in the Soviet Union. What do you plan to do, comrade?"

Mike replied, "We have decided to sue the Gaming Board and try to get the court to reverse their decision. And since your letter of support to the Gaming Board was the best one that we received, we'd like you to testify at the trial."

"Holy moly," I said. "That might be difficult. But let me tell you my situation. I'm the chief financial officer of Burson-Marsteller, a large marketing communication and public affairs firm, and we've got serious problems with our business in Europe. My senior European finance team is based in London. Therefore, I have been making frequent trips to London, and that should continue for some time. Is there any way that we could somehow coordinate a court appearance with my travel schedule? I'd be willing to give you an hour or two, but I can't justify a special trip to London to testify."

"That's great," said Mike. "I'm sure that we can work something out. We'll be happy to pay for your airfare and to provide you with a room at the Ritz. We'd also like to compensate you for your time."

"Not on your life," I replied. "I'm coming over on a necessary business trip anyway, so you are not causing me any additional expense except for maybe a taxi ride or two. And you can't pay me for my time. If the Gaming Board lawyer ever asks me how much you guys are paying me, I want to be able to say 'not one schilling.' Otherwise, I will lose all credibility. All I want out of this is that, should we win, I want to be member 00001 at the new Ritz Club."

"It's a deal," Mike said.

The trial at the Magistrates' Court took place in December 1997. Mike had arranged for me to testify first, at 9:00 a.m., so I could get back to my office as quickly as possible. Never having testified in a British court, I admit that I was a little nervous. But when I was called to the witness box, I looked up at the three-magistrate panel, and all trepidation ended. This was going to be a blast!

I testified for about a half hour, with all the questions and answers that you would expect: my background, my use of the club, why it should be reopened. One exchange is worth noting in detail. It concerned my use of the club:

> Barrister: "How often would you say that you frequent the Ritz Club?"

> Me: "Well, that all depends on how often I travel to London. Some years it is fifteen or twenty times; other years it is only four or five."

Barrister: "Would it surprise you to learn that, according to our records, you visited the Ritz Club only twice in all of 1996?"

Me: "Your records must be in error. I'm sure that I was there many more times than that."

Barrister: "I believe that our records are correct, sir. Isn't it true that you were a relatively infrequent user of the club?"

Me: "I'm sorry, but your data is clearing wrong." [turning to the magistrates] "Your Honors, I keep a record of every visit to the Ritz Club, as well as a tally on my winnings and losings. May I consult it?"

Head Magistrate: "Go right ahead, Mr. Krauss."

Me [after pulling out my diary]: "Let's see, in 1996, I visited the club on February 10 and 11, March 25, May 15, 16, and 17, July 8, July 23. Do you want me to keep going? Just scanning the list, it looks like I visited the club maybe twelve times that year. And if you're interested, my net winnings for the year were £4,350."

Barrister: "No further questions."

After I left the witness box, I received sincere thanks from Mike Steele and from Sir Edward and Sir William. "I hope that I helped," I said. "The only thing that troubled me was that the magistrates and the barristers weren't wearing white wigs. I was so hoping for wigs."

"They only wear wigs in the High Court," Mike said.

"Sorry," Sir William added.

I didn't hear a thing for maybe three months. Then I got another call from Mike Steele. "We lost," he said, "but we are appealing it to the High Court. Will you testify again?"

"I will," I said. "But only if the judges have white wigs. If they don't have wigs, you will owe me £1,000,000."

"It's a deal! Let me know your schedule, and I'll get it coordinated with one of your trips."

I think it was maybe April when I finally appeared in front of the High Court. When I stepped into the witness box, I looked across into the gallery. There was Mike Steele pointing to his head and mouthing the words "Wigs! Wigs!" Sure enough, all five of the High Court judges had on one of those dashing white wigs. There went my £1,000,000.

This time my testimony lasted about forty minutes. It was pretty much a rerun of the Magistrates' Court, except for one exchange. I was beginning to run out of patience with the insistence by the government that one more casino license should not be granted. I interrupted the proceedings and said to the judges, "I'm an American, and I'm not exactly sure how things work over here. Am I allowed to address the court on my own?"

The senior judge responded, "Mr. Krauss, if you have something that you want to say, go ahead and say it."

Best I can remember, here is what I said:

> If it pleases the court, I don't understand why we are here. There are at least fifty people in this courtroom trying to deny or to allow or to decide on a casino license for the Ritz Club, a club that I should point out has been an iconic landmark in London for many years. Exactly what problem are we trying to solve here? Is there concern that Sir William and Sir Edward will lose all their money?

Is there concern that the moral fiber of the citizens of London will be weakened?

I understand that London Clubs International is worried that if the license is approved, they won't make as much money since they decided to locate only two blocks away from the Ritz Club. But isn't that the nature of capitalism and free enterprise?

In my country, if I chose to open a shoe store right next door to an existing shoe store, there is not a Shoe Store Commission that can stop me. I'm allowed by US law to do as many stupid things as I can afford to pay for. Thank you for letting me get all this off of my chest.

Most of the time that I was speaking, I noticed that the judges were trying to cover their mouths and suppress laughs. But they did succeed in preserving their dignity.

Shortly after that, I was excused. In the hallway outside the courtroom, I was met by Mike, Sir Edward, and Sir William. All three were jubilant. Sir Edward said to me, "Kurt, how can we possibly repay you?"

Sir Edward was one of the richest men in England and was a bachelor with no children. "Sir Edward," I said, "why don't you adopt me? You and I could cut a swath through this country!"

Both he and his brother started giggling in that high-pitched, tittery, English gentleman's giggle. They didn't seem to realize that I was dead serious.

The next person to testify was my close friend and partner of twenty years, Horst Metz. He was also a high-stakes blackjack player, and he and I had gambled together many times over the years. We often met at the Ritz Club.

Horst answered many of the same questions I had answered. But he was able to work in yet another argument in favor of granting the Ritz Club a license: that the competition among high-end casinos was global in nature. He spoke of his experiences in casinos in Europe and Asia and how the Ritz Club was actually a destination for many international players. If it were to stay closed, it was not at all clear that these customers would naturally move to another London casino. And if they didn't, the British casino industry would be worse off.

The High Court decided against the Gaming Board and ordered them to grant a license to the Ritz Club. According to Mike Steele, their written opinion used a number of Horst's and my arguments.

A few weeks later, I received six magnums of champagne from Sir William and Sir Edward. And I did become member 00001 at the new Ritz Club, which opened in August 1998. I'm still hoping for the adoption.

Fast Eddie hopes that you enjoyed the book and leaves you with the thought that we only regret the chances we didn't take.

Printed in the United States
By Bookmasters